52
F L O R I D A
weekends

52
FLORIDA
weekends

Janet & Gordon Groene

COUNTRY ROADS PRESS
Oaks • Pennsylvania

52 Florida Weekends

© 1996 by Janet Groene with Gordon Groene. All rights reserved.

Published by Country Roads Press
P.O. Box 838, 2170 West Drive
Oaks, PA 19456

Text design by Studio 3.
Illustrations by Dale Ingrid Swensson.
Map by Allen Crider.
Typesetting by Typeworks.

ISBN 1-56626-129-5

Library of Congress Cataloging-in-Publication Data

Groene, Janet.
   52 Florida weekends / Janet Groene, with Gordon Groene ;
illustrator, Dale Ingrid Swensson.
      p.   cm.
   Includes index.
   ISBN 1-56626-129-5
   1. FloridaTours.   I. Groene, Gordon. II. Title.
F309.3.G749 1995
917.5904'63–dc20   95-10459
                                         CIP

Printed in the United States of America.
10 9 8 7 6 5 4 3 2 1

To memories of Bonnie and Archie Gann
of Merritt Island, Florida,
who flew away together January 16, 1993.
Theirs was a love story.

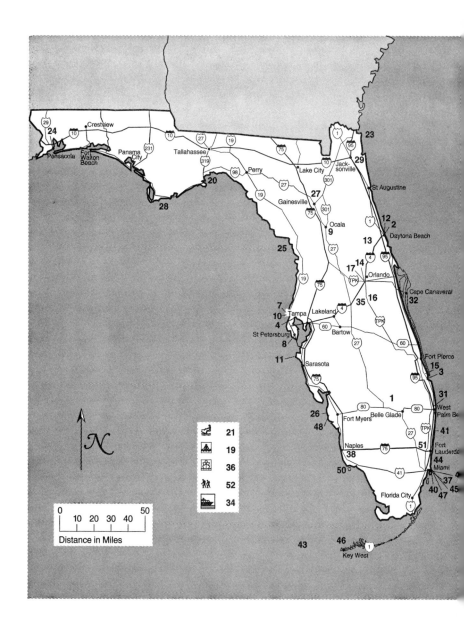

Crestview
29
24
10
Pensacola
Fort Walton Beach
Panama City
231
Tallahassee
319
27
19
75
10
Jacksonville
23
1
95
29
St Augustine
98
Perry
27
Lake City
301
28
20
19
27
Gainesville
27
75
301
Ocala
9
12
1
2
Daytona Beach
13
25
27
4
95
17 14
TPK
Orlando
32
Cape Canaveral
7
10
4
Tampa
Lakeland
35 16
St Petersburg
60
4
TPK
8
Bartow
60
Fort Pierce
11
Sarasota
27
15 3
75
95
1
31
26
80
Belle Glade
80
West Palm Be
48
Fort Myers
27
TPK
41
Naples
51
Fort Lauderda
38
75
44
50
41
Miami
37
Florida City
40 47 45
1
43
46
Key West
1

21
19
36
52
34

N

0   50
10 20 30 40
Distance in Miles

Contents

Introduction   *xi*

Spring

1. **Circling the Big Waters**, Lake Okeechobee   *1*
2. **On the Sweet Side**, Daytona   *5*
3. **Discover the Flapper Era**, Stuart   *7*
4. **Grand Resorts Restored**, St. Petersburg/Clearwater   *10*
5. **Go to the Dogs**   *13*
6. **Out of Africa**, Busch Gardens/Tampa   *16*
7. **Especially on Sunday**, Tarpon Springs   *19*
8. **Elegant Art Mecca**, St. Petersburg   *21*
9. **Horse Around**, Ocala   *23*
10. **Tartans and Tattoos**, Dunedin   *26*
11. **In Love with Anna Maria**   *29*
12. **Speed, Speed, Speed**, Daytona   *32*
13. **Discover Bassin'**, DeLand   *35*
14. **Movie Mania**, Orlando   *38*

Summer

15. **Sample a Club Med Evening**   *43*
16. **A Ridin', Ropin' Rodeo Weekend**, Kissimmee   *46*
17. **A Fairytale Wedding**, Walt Disney World   *50*

18. Harvest Nature's Plenty   53
19. Make a Splash in a Water Park   56
20. A Summer at Seaside   58
21. A Waterskiing Weekend   60
22. Canoe the True Florida   63
23. Summer's Isle, Amelia Island   66
24. The Emerald Coast, Pensacola   70
25. Where the Sun Meets Sea, Cedar Key   73
26. Rough It on a Barrier Island, Cayo Costa   75
27. Take a Collegiate Break, Gainesville   78
28. The World's Your Oyster, Apalachicola   81

Fall

29. Beyond the Gator Bowl, Jacksonville   85
30. Make Friends with a Manatee   88
31. Plush Pleasures of the Palm Beaches   92
32. Lost in Space   95
33. From Cigars to Soho, Ybor City   99
34. Exploring by Houseboat, St. Johns River   103
35. Dogfight in the Skies, Kissimmee   106
36. Weekend to Weekend, The Love Boat   108
37. Monkey Around in Miami   111

Winter

38. Next to Nature in Naples   117
39. Everglades à la Carte   120
40. Coral Gables Goes Global   122
41. Boca Beyond the Beach   125
42. Deco Nights, Haute Couture Days   128
43. Islands in the Stream, Dry Tortugas   131
44. Where Is Aventura?   135
45. Doral Golf Resort and Spa, Miami   137
46. Catch Conch Fever, Key West   140
47. Moon Over Miami   143
48. The Islands of Pine Island Sound   146
49. A Looney Tunes™ Weekend   149
50. One in Ten Thousand, Marco Island   152
51. Sunny Sunday Jazz Brunch, Fort Lauderdale   155
52. Happy Trails to You   158

Index   161

Introduction

What is your idea of the perfect place for the two of you to steal away for a weekend? Whether you are a job-jangled working couple, or harried parents who need to recharge your romance with a weekend all to yourselves, or an older couple who never tire of exploring new vistas together, this book is for you.

Florida's weekend smorgasbord is rich in coastal sweetmeats, in forest feasts for the eyes and ears, in sophisticated cities, rollicking festivals, and a cultural mix that could be called a piquant paella.

Play it lazy, splaying on the sands at a beachfront resort. Or go for an athletic high with a vigorous weekend of sailing, scuba diving, blue-water sportfishing, tennis, or a spa program. For sports spectators, Florida is the scene of nationally famous tennis and golf tournaments, bowl games, auto racing at Daytona, and spring training matches for major league baseball teams.

Splurge at a luxury hotel and have dinner in a different, world-class restaurant each night. Take a luxury cruise out of a Florida port. Or pitch a tent under a loblolly pine in a state forest and spend evenings around the campfire roasting marshmallows and strumming a guitar.

Highbrow pursuits include opera, ballet, theater, and standout museums. Or let your hair down at a chickee bar or at the swamp buggy races. Line dance at a country nightclub and eat your fill of blue crabs, served in dishpans atop newspaper-covered tables.

Disappear on a houseboat, a remote island, a canoe-in campsite deep in the Everglades. Or make the scene among crowds of international cognoscenti at jazz clubs, discos, juried art shows, and polo matches.

Florida is a waterfront wonderland that faces on the Atlantic, the Gulf of Mexico, and countless miles of lakes, bays, and rivers. Its central highlands are rolling green hills threaded with country lanes and timeless villages. It's bracketed by the old: St. Augustine and Pensacola in the north, and Key West's gracious Victoriana at its southern tip. And by the new: glittering high-rise condos in Miami and neo-Victoriana at Seaside, the model planned community in the Panhandle.

Florida's major airports are less than four hours from most points in the United States. Take the overnight train from New Orleans or New York. Or come by bus or car or RV. Just get here, and let the sands and sunshine do the rest.

SEASON TO TASTE

Although many people think of Florida as a winter getaway, more tourists actually visit the Sunshine State in summer. One reason is that families can travel only when children are out of school. Summer is also the water sports season in south Florida, when Floridians themselves vacation on their boats. Thanks to lower rates in south Florida in summer, resorts fill up with conferences and bargain seekers.

The reverse is true in the Emerald Coast beach resorts of the Panhandle and the Discovery Coast at St. Augustine and Jacksonville, where summer is the more expensive high season. It's usually too cold in winter for swimming but perfect for tennis, golf, bicycling, and other active sports at low-season room rates.

September can be exceptionally wet and humid; summer in the Everglades brings clouds of mosquitoes; winter cold fronts can occasionally freeze Orlando and chill Miami. Nevertheless, while this book has been divided according to four seasons, almost any time is the right time to visit any destination listed in these pages.

1 Circling the Big Waters
Lake Okeechobee

In a simple, 150-mile drive around Lake Okeechobee, you'll see one of Florida's most fascinating, underexplored destinations. The Florida Division of Tourism guidebook barely mentions it, yet Okeechobee is the second-largest freshwater lake in the United States.

The Big Waters have captivated visitors since the Conquistadores, but today they're little known except to bass anglers. Start at the city of Okeechobee, then go south on State 700, then State 78 through Lakeport to Moore Haven, east on US 27 to Clewiston and Belle Glade, then north on State 715 to Pahokee, and take US 441 back to Okeechobee. It's a perfect two- or three-day weekend jaunt.

A vast saucer of water, Lake Okeechobee once drained the 3,000-square-mile Kissimmee River Basin and spilled over from its south shore into the Everglades. Woods and waters were alive with otters and panthers, fish and alligators. Prehistoric Indian tribes thrived here, dug canals by hand, then vanished. The lake was mentioned by sixteenth-century Spanish explorers, but modern history didn't begin until the Seminole wars when the army built forts around the shoreline. They're gone now, but old blazes found on cypress trees are dated in the early 1800s.

Mankind's first attempt to tame the lake came after the Civil War, when a developer dug canals to connect Lake Okeechobee with Kissimmee to the north and the Gulf of Mexico to the West. Settlers could now arrive by boat, and by 1905 the O.K. Fish Company was harvesting catfish by the ton. The state began dredging in 1910, and the ecological balance of the region was changed forever.

In the community of Okeechobee, which was laid out in the flamboyant Flagler railroad era, see the stately 1917 courthouse and quaint downtown shops and cafés. Then drive north on US 98 and look for the museum, a typical Cracker schoolhouse.

Driving southwest, cross the Kissimmee River and pass miles of meadows where huge herds of cattle graze among seas of black-eyed Susans along Fisheating Creek. Lakeport, now just a memory on the map, was a flourishing settlement of Belgian and Polish immigrants until it was wiped out in the 1926 hurricane. At Moore Haven, you can launch a boat, fish, take shots of the stately old courthouse, and imagine the scene here in 1926 when more than 200 people drowned in a hurricane.

After you cross the Caloosahatchee River, meadows give way to fields of sugarcane. Clewiston, the "sweetest little town in America," has a first-rate museum with relics from the Seminole and sugar eras, plus memorabilia from the early 1940s when British pilots trained near here. The Union Jack still flies over a British-owned cemetery where their dead are buried.

Built in 1938, the charming Clewiston Inn is a good place to overnight or dine. Don't miss the wildlife mural, painted in 1945. Drive on to Belle Glade, where a 1928 hurricane drowned 2,000 people. A sculpture in front of the library on

South Main Street sums up the horror in its depiction of a family fleeing before the lake's rising waters.

Lake Harbor is now just a speck on the map, but it was from the roof of the Bolles Hotel here that eager suckers looked out over the lake and bought submerged land on the promise that it would be drained. The project was foiled by the hurricanes of '26 and '28 and the stock market crash of 1929.

Cross the one-lane wooden bridge to the Belle Glade Marina and Campground and play a round of miniature golf. The Drawbridge Cafe at the bridge serves authentic Cracker fare in a sunny setting. Continue along the dike to Pahokee, with its rows of royal palms. Settled after World War I in a feverish grab for the rich mucklands, its remnants from the glory days include a grand bank (1922) and an abandoned Art Deco–era school. Stately homes along the road once were on the lake; today they overlook only the stark, forty-two-foot-high Herbert Hoover Dike. At Port Mayaca, fish the St. Lucie canal for fresh and salt water species. From here US 441 winds back to your starting point at Okeechobee.

The best sightseeing around the lake is at thirty-nine free parks marked Dike Access. Most have picnic tables, rest rooms, and launch ramps; some have campgrounds, marinas, and other facilities as well as historic markers or displays related to the lake's booms and busts.

Specifically: Request a brochure and map from the Natural Resources Office, 525 Ridgelawn Road, Clewiston, FL 33440-5399, and the brochure Lakefront Legacy from the Florida Endowment for the Humanities, 1718 East 7th Avenue #301, Tampa, FL 33605. Okeechobee KOA is a complete camping resort with restaurant, golf, tennis, tent and RV sites, and bunkhouses called Kamping Kabins, 800-845-6846. Clewiston KOA is also a full-service campground with Kamping Kabins, 813-983-7078. The Clewiston Inn, 813-983-8151, offers weekend packages.

2 On the Sweet Side
Daytona

The savage Seminole wars, which have never been settled by treaty, raged off and on in Florida from 1818 through 1858. In one fiery rampage in the 1830s, all the sugar plantations in east central Florida were burned to rubble. It was said that every house south of St. Augustine was burned to the ground.

For years, thickets and scrub forest covered what had once been lush plantations. Now turned into parks, they are pleasant, wilderness sites where you can eat a picnic lunch, stroll among the ruins and hike nature trails, and imagine what Florida was like during its lusty plantation era. In one weekend you can easily visit the following parks.

Sugar Mill Gardens
New Smyrna Beach
A New York partnership bought 2,600 acres here in 1830, planted them to sugarcane, and sent refined sugar by the shipload to the tables of New England, Europe, and Britain. When the Seminoles attacked in 1835, desperate settlers poled and paddled their way north on the Halifax River to find safety at Bulowville, which was itself burned a year later. What remains is a collage of ruins and rambling gardens.

Sugar Mill Gardens
Port Orange
The plantation goes back to 1804, when 995 acres here were planted by a Bahamian who was later killed by Indians. Under its new owner, it was burned in 1836. Only a few walls and a tangle of machinery remained, but the sugar mill was rebuilt, and by 1851, using new steam engines, it was producing 200 tons of raw sugar a year. That ended with the Civil War. Soldiers camped on the abandoned property during the

war and produced salt, a desperately needed food preservative, by boiling seawater in the big vats. Then the site was
abandoned again and forgotten until the late 1940s when it
was turned into a primitive theme park named Bongoland.

Enormous concrete dinosaurs still stand incongruously
among nineteenth-century machinery, empty foundations,
and lone chimneys. Today the placid twelve-acre park con-
tains extensive botanical gardens and picnic sites as well as
the ruins and the dinosaurs. A photographer's delight, it's
often chosen for fashion shoots because of the variety of
backgrounds.

Bulow Plantation State Historic Site

In the early 1820s, Major Charles Bulow's slaves began clear-
ing his 4,600 acres along a creek west of what is now Flagler
Beach and planted them to sugar, cotton, rice, and indigo. By
1831 a thriving and gracious plantation, Bulowville played
host to nature artist John James Audubon. A few years later, it
was a smoldering ruin. Its young owner, Major Bulow's son
John, fled to Paris, where he died heartbroken at the age of
twenty-six. On the site today, see the remains of the house
site, slave quarters, and mill along Bulow Creek, which is also
a state canoe trail.

Specifically: Contact the Daytona Convention and Visitors Bureau, 126 East Orange Avenue, Daytona Beach, FL
32114, 800-854-1234 or 904-255-0415. Southeast Volusia
Chamber of Commerce, 115 Canal Street, New Smyrna Beach,
FL 32168, 800-541-9621 or 904-428-2449. Ask for information about sugar mill ruins, accommodations, dining, and
local maps. Bulow Creek State Park, 3351 Old Dixie Highway,
Ormond Beach, FL 32174. All sites are open during daylight
hours. Some have a modest admission charge.

3 Discover the Flapper Era
Stuart

In the Roaring Twenties land speculators poured into the Sunshine State. Citrus harvests were worth millions, and easy money grew on palm trees. By the Crash of 1929, the party was over. A little-known place to rediscover the everyday flavor of Florida's 1920s flapper era is in Stuart, a pretty riverfront city between Cape Canaveral and the Gold Coast.

Like many Florida cities along the Atlantic, Stuart bulged west to find room for neighborhoods and malls and stretched east to build high-rise condos on the beach. Historic downtowns that were for decades the heart of such communities were all or partially abandoned. Today many are being revitalized as Florida Main Street cities.

Stuart, with more than three square blocks of 1920s storefronts, is one of the success stories of the program. Check into an oceanfront resort such as the Mobil Four-Star, AAA Four-Diamond Indian River Plantation for the weekend. You'll have the best of the Hutchinson Island beach, a hotel room or a villa with full kitchen, a choice of restaurants and lounges with live entertainment, swimming pools, a marina with boat rentals and a sightseeing cruise, bicycle rentals, and a choice of four great golf courses. It's a supersize resort, all tied together with a free tram system.

Plan to spend at least a day discovering the old downtown, and longer for festivals or a special show at the restored 1926 movie palace. A quick jog off US 1 brings you to Confusion Corner, a jagged intersection where four wagon paths converged in the days when farmers brought their pineapple harvests into town for shipment north on the railroad.

The downtown streetscape consists of a couple of streets around a small traffic circle centered with an Italian fountain titled Abundance. Sit on a park bench to watch the fountain or take a table under the awning at the Jolly Sailor and order a gin and tonic.

This is a Main Street straight out of Mayberry, with a cast of characters ranging from grizzled beach bums to platinum-coiffed fashion plates. There are shops, but it's no Worth Avenue, historic buildings, but it's no St. Augustine, people watching, but it's no Key West. Downtown Stuart is pleasantly normal, 1920s style.

Shops along one side of Osceola Street run all the way through to Seminole, so you can thread your way up the street by browsing an antique shop front to rear, then enter the next boutique or gallery and shop your way back to Osceola, and so on.

Linger at Rare Earth Pottery to watch David and Diana Engesath at work, then choose a piece of their signed, hand-thrown pottery. Their Christian Collection, including David's famous Everlasting Light oil lamp, is increasingly collectible. Smells from the Osceola Bakery will take you back to grand-mother's kitchen. Pick up crusty sweet rolls and herbed breads for a future picnic, or get a sack of butter cookies to eat on the River Walk as you watch an endless flotilla of boats fizz by.

The Post Office Arcade on the other side of Osceola Street was a grand innovation when it was opened in 1925. A dogleg design draws cooling breezes through a corridor that opens onto shops, an indoor sidewalk café, and a Book Nook that has one of the best Florida sections in the area. All that remains of the old post office itself is a bank of brass boxes still set into a wall.

Don't miss Stuart Feed Supply along the River Walk. It's not only a fine example of Wood Frame Vernacular design; it's still a real store selling real merchandise. The building also houses a fledgling museum with displays depicting

Stuart history in the days when Indians came to trade otter and raccoon hides at this very store.

Fine restaurants thrive downtown now that it's again the "in" place to hang out. Ashley's, located in an old bank, is named for the Ashley gang that once held up the bank. Coffee and Sweets serves fancy coffees and ice creams, and sells dozens of flavors of specialty coffees and candies. Nature's Way and the Flagler Grill are lunchtime favorites.

The Jolly Sailor is an upscale pub, filled with Cunard memorabilia and owned by a British merchant seaman who likes nothing better than regaling his guests with tales about his seafaring adventures. Peek out the side entrance at the old Austin taxicab that is parked there, then order a pint and a plowman's lunch. Eat typical pub grub such as bubble and squeak or bangers and mash, or sit in a cozy booth to dine on Dover sole or prime steaks.

Straight out of the jazz age, Stuart is a quiet getaway to enjoy any time of year.

Specifically: Indian River Plantation, 800-444-3389 or 407-225-6990. Ask about packages. Embassy Suites Resort, 800-328-2289 or 407-863-4000. For a walking map of downtown Stuart, write the Chamber of Commerce, 1650 South Kanner Highway, Stuart, FL 34994, 407-287-1088 or 800-524-9704. Ask about hot dates. Occasional concerts bring in thousands of visitors to an otherwise sleepy downtown.

4 Grand Resorts Restored
St. Petersburg/Clearwater

The Victorian era brought railroad lines to Florida, resulting in a splendid growth spurt in an exotic, unknown wilderness where few roads existed. Today three of the grandest resorts of the Gulf coast, all of them built to serve affluent northerners who arrived by rail to spend the winter, have been lavishly restored, air-conditioned, and opened to a year-round clientele of nostalgia seekers.

The Stouffer Vinoy in downtown St. Petersburg, the Don CeSar Beach Resort on St. Pete Beach, and the Belleview Mido Resort Hotel in Clearwater have several features in common. All are on the National Register of Historic Places. All are built with rare woods that are no longer available, such as heart pine and pecky cypress. All are in the luxury price range, although off-season packages are a bargain.

They all offer all the amenities of first-class resorts: fine restaurants that have a loyal local following, golf privileges, tennis, activities, old-world service, sprawling grounds filled with tropical flowers and greenery, swimming pools, spa services, and croquet and other lawn games that were popular in the Gatsby era. All offer brief historic tours. Take them; they're part of the "insider" fun and romance of rediscovering a bygone era.

The Don CeSar, the only one on the beach, is a magnificent pile of pink stucco and distinctive towers that can be seen for miles out to sea. Turned into a hospital for airmen during World War II, it has been restored and re-restored to new heights of comfort and luxury. Sail or windsurf off the beach, play tennis on sea-breeze-cooled courts, and shop the swank boutiques.

The Belleview Mido is on a bluff overlooking the bay. An enormous, three-story sprawl of endless corridors, gables, attics, and cellars, the "White Queen of the Gulf" is one of the largest wooden hotels in the world. Swim in indoor or outdoor pools or take the free shuttle to Clearwater Beach. Free shuttles also serve the resort's own Cabana Club on Sand Key, where it's fun to spend the day and stay on for dinner in the evening. Laze in the pool and Jacuzzi, then retire to the cozy restaurant and lounge to watch the sun sink into the Gulf of Mexico.

The Stouffer Vinoy is in downtown St. Petersburg, handy to that city's cultural treasures, including the Dali Museum, the new Florida International Museum, one of the nation's best children's museums, and the Pier with its aquarium and restaurants-shops complex. Don't miss the historic museum at the Pier. Housed here is the tiny airboat that flew the nation's first scheduled air route in the days when it took hours to travel by railroad between Tampa and St. Pete. In the two-seater airboat, skimming barely above the sea, the trip took only twenty minutes.

So elite were the guests in this regal, Mediterranean Revival showplace that the Vinoy prospered even during the depression. The Biddles of Philadelphia stayed here. So did the Smiths of Smith-Corona, Babe Ruth, F. Scott Fitzgerald, Alf Landon, Herbert Hoover, and the Pillsburys. When the Vinoy Park Hotel opened in 1925, rates were among the highest in the state – $20 nightly including meals. For years it sat empty, eluding the wrecker's ball, and now it is once again the city's showplace.

Try all these historic hotels any time, but especially in November when days are warm and clear, rates are at rock bottom, and the Kahlua Cup Regatta brings a hundred yachts to Clearwater from all over the world to race a 127-nautical-mile course.

Perhaps best of all in this look at historic yesterdays are

the old railroad routes, which now form a forty-seven-mile walking, jogging, and bicycling trail that stretches the entire length of Pinellas County from park to park. Bring your rollerblades, bicycle, or jogging shoes and see how much of the trail you can cover. It's open during daylight hours; no motorized vehicles are allowed.

Specifically: For information about the Kahlua Cup, contact the Chamber of Commerce, 813-461-0011; the Belleview Mido Resort Hotel, 813-442-6171; Don CeSar Beach Resort, 813-360-1881; Stouffer Vinoy Resort, 813-894-1000.

5 Go to the Dogs

Greyhound racing is the sixth-largest spectator sport in America. Even if the two of you don't follow it as a sport and even if you don't gamble, look at it as an exciting and offbeat way to spend a sporty weekend without spending a fortune on admission tickets. Florida, with eighteen tracks around the state and three in Jacksonville alone, is the doggonedest racing state in the nation.

Among the oldest and most respected breeds in the canine kingdom, greyhounds were so revered in the early Arab world that the birth of a new dog rated second only to the birth of a son—well above the arrival of a daughter. King Canute of England decreed in A.D. 1014 that greyhounds were too noble to be owned by common folk. Only those of royal blood were allowed to use them in hunting.

The dogs aren't all grey, by the way. They come in all colors. The name, it is thought, may have evolved from the term gazehound, because they chase what they see, not what they smell.

It was a plague of jackrabbits that brought greyhounds to North America late in the nineteenth century. As farmers watched their dogs chase the rabbits, they began boasting about whose dog was fastest. Boasting became betting. When the first mechanical rabbit was invented in 1912 and a track was opened in California in 1919, dog racing was officially off and running. Today the sport is found in nineteen states and attracts 30 million attendees a year.

Let's look at your weekend getaway from two viewpoints. Do you want to wager, or are you nongamblers who simply want to soak up the excitement and speed of racing?

FOR GAMBLERS

With purses that can go into six figures, pari-mutuel wagering is big business in Florida. A Tampa fan won $1.1 million in 1985; a greyhound commanded a stud fee of $500,000 in 1987. In each evening or matinee session you can bet on as many as fifteen races, perhaps parlaying one bet into a fortune. Some of the dog tracks also have television and computer tie-ins with a horse track. Through electronic magic, you can play the dogs and the ponies all at once.

Track operators do everything possible to make it easy to make bets. Hostesses circulate constantly, available to help newcomers understand the how and why of Trifectas and Superfectas. If you're still not confident, place your bet at a Help window where you won't be rushed. Many tracks have videos, clinics, seminars, and classes too, all of them free.

FOR SPECTATORS

If you aren't interested in wagering, you probably won't become dog track regulars. You will, however, be surprised at the quirky fun of a weekend at the races. The first surprise is the prices. The big money is made on wagering, so everything else is sold at little more than cost. You pay only a token admission to sit in the open stands; admission to the heated, air-conditioned clubhouse may be only a dollar or two. For another couple of dollars, you can enjoy valet parking.

Plush and upscale, clubhouses have friendly cocktail lounges and fine, full-service dining at surprisingly modest prices. While you dine on prime rib or fresh seafood, watch the races through big glass windows or on your own tableside television set. Between races, tune the set to the horse track simulcast or to the station of your choice. The dogs run as fast as 45 mph, so each race is over in minutes, but the racing serves as a sideline to the color, pageantry, the passion of the wagering, the parading of the dogs, and the party atmosphere of the clubhouse.

Perhaps the best feature for animal lovers is the greyhound adoption program at some Florida tracks. Usually, the adoptable dogs are retired racers, although a puppy is occasionally available when it's obvious that it has no future in racing or breeding. Docile house pets who can spend most of the day curled up like cats, greyhounds are sight-driven, so they must be walked on a leash or kept in a well-fenced yard because, once lost, they may not be able to find the way home. They're quiet, loving, undemanding, and make excellent pets.

Adoptive homes are closely screened, and adoptions are followed up later to make sure the animal is being well cared for. A fee of about $100 is charged to pay for shots, neutering, and any other care the dog needs.

Specifically: Contact the American Greyhound Track Operators Association, 1065 N.E. 125th Street, Suite 219, North Miami, FL 33161, 305-893-2101. Request a list of Florida greyhound tracks and their schedules. Some are open all year, others only during certain months. Call ahead for lunch or dinner reservations. For information on the Adopt a Greyhound program, call 800-366-1472. A recorded message will ask for your name and address; details will be sent to you.

6 Out of Africa
Busch Gardens/Tampa

Florida insiders have a secret that rushed tourists never discover. It is that the state's best theme parks and most alluring attractions are worth visiting not just once, but time and again. Many locals buy year-round passes to their favorite parks and return sometimes weekly or even daily to see the changing gardens, new shows, and animal antics, and enjoy the great people watching provided by the crowds that stream through these parks.

Walt Disney World, Cypress Gardens, Sea World, Universal Studios, and Busch Gardens offer tremendous variety in floral displays, fireworks, rides, comedy acts, street characters, razzle-dazzle shows, quiet rambles, dining and snacking, new and changing exhibits, and constant surprises.

At all of them, summer flowers give way in autumn to seas of brilliant mums and geraniums. Christmas creates new spectacles of winking lights and happy song. Springtime brings blossoms galore and a rush of tender new leaves. In summer, these parks offer icy drinks, splashing waterfalls, and the shade of gingko trees and gumbo-limbos while you wait for the next show to start.

Busch Gardens is a living, changing park to immerse yourself in time and again. Come for the weekend, buy a two- or three-day pass, and give it a chance to get under your skin. You're strolling along when suddenly a band comes blaring down the street, dressed in smart bush uniforms. Or a belly dancer glides through the crowds accompanied by cymbals and drums. Animals are in constant motion, beguiling those who stop to watch by the hour.

Busch Gardens is packed with animal habitats of all kinds from a petting zoo to a veldt where some 500 zebras, giraffes, and other African species roam free. Apes and chimps have their own world; some observers can't tear themselves away from this section. Other habitats house bald eagles, koala bears, white Bengal tigers, exotic parrots, bottle-nosed dolphins, and more.

More than a garden and more than a zoo, Busch Gardens is home to more than 3,300 animals. In addition, it is an amusement park where Kumba, one of the fastest and highest roller coasters in the Southeast, hits speeds of 60 mph and more. Scream through a ride on the Scorpion. Take a water safari on the Tanganyika Tidal Wave, the Stanley Falls log flume, or the Congo River Rapids.

Shows, which go on through the day, feature the world's most talented acrobats, ice skaters, aerialists, magicians, dancers, and other artists. Have a free beer at the hospitality center, where you can also see the famous Clydesdale horses. Have dinner at the Victorian-theme Crown Colony or the lively Das Festhaus. Shop the bazaars.

Catch a show at Marrakesh or the Moroccan Palace. Coo over newborns at the Nairobi Field Station animal nursery. Ride the monorail, the sky ride, and the choo-choo. Taken as a long and leisurely weekend, Busch Gardens goes beyond theme park. This is nineteenth-century Africa in living color, earthy and romantic. You'll enjoy it from Stanleyville to Timbuktu.

Specifically: Take the Busch Boulevard exit off I-275 and go east two miles. For more information, contact Busch Gardens, Box 9158, Tampa, FL 33674, 813-987-5000. Ask about a two- or three-day pass and about special events such as riding the feed truck or taking a camera safari. Many budget-class chain motels are found along I-275, but the

Colony Hotel at the Busch Boulevard exit is both the closest resort to Busch Gardens and an upscale hotel with tennis, indoor and outdoor pools, sauna, workout room, room service, lounge with live entertainment, and restaurant. For reservations, 800-777-1700 or 813-933-4011.

7 Especially on Sunday
Tarpon Springs

Even today, the sun-drenched downtown streets of Tarpon Springs could pass for a Mediterranean seaside village. Deep in the shady patio of a coffee shop, men argue politics in Greek over tiny cups of strong brew. Sponges spill out of bins in a street vendor's stall along Dodecanese Boulevard. On cool evenings, lovers stroll under starlit skies, stopping for ouzo in a flower-rimmed courtyard.

Strolling the boulevard is, in fact, one of the simplest and most colorful pleasures of this waterfront village north of Tampa. Have a Greek salad at Louis Pappas's Riverside. Stop at a sidewalk take-away for a slab of baklava, shop in curio shops for Greek lace and pottery, and sit in the shade overlooking the river to watch the passing parade of workboats and pleasure craft.

The historic Sponge Exchange sells more souvenirs than sponges these days, but there are enough barrels spilling over with natural sponges of all kinds to give the Exchange the same look it had in the early 1900s when divers from the Aegean came here to harvest the largest sponge beds in the Americas. By 1905, two hundred sponge boats were operating here. Antique diving equipment and a typical sponge boat are on display, reminders of an industry that was decimated when disease destroyed many of the sponge beds. By the time they recovered, synthetic sponges were in vogue.

Today some sponges are still harvested, and are sold twice a week at sponge auctions that are held in the Greek manner using silent, written bids. Ride the sponge-diving exhibition boat on a short cruise of the Anclote River to get the true feel of this ancient industry.

At no time does the sun shine more brightly and Greek pride burn more brilliantly than on the religious holiday

Epiphany. On the sixth day of January, people come from all over the world to view the traditional ceremonies, which begin with a four-hour matins service. Then a white dove of peace is released and a golden cross is thrown into Spring Bayou. Young men dive to retrieve it, the finder is assured a year filled with blessings, and the day proceeds with feasting and dancing in true Zorba style.

St. Nicholas Greek Orthodox church, still a center of village life, is a treasury of Byzantine art and architecture. Built in 1943, it's a replica of St. Sophia in Constantinople. Visitors are welcome every day of the year. Art lovers will also want to drop by the Universalist Church to see the world's largest collection of paintings by American landscape artist, George Inness Sr., whose most notable paintings were done in the Tarpon Springs area. It's closed June through September.

Stay at Spring Bayou, a bed and breakfast near the sponge docks. Or book a villa at Innisbrook, one of Florida's largest resorts. It has restaurants, lounges, tennis, golf courses galore, a stocked fishing lake, wooded hiking paths, and all the other features of a fine, four-star resort.

Specifically: Request information about accommodations and special events from the Chamber of Commerce, 210 South Pinellas Avenue, Tarpon Springs, FL 34689, 813-937-6109. If you're coming for the Epiphany celebration, book well in advance because this is one of the largest Greek festivals outside Greece.

8 Elegant Art Mecca
St. Petersburg

At the turn of the century, St. Petersburg was one of Florida's in spots for winter crowds, who arrived with piles of steamer trunks and stayed all season. The world's first scheduled airline flew between Tampa and St. Pete in 1914, carrying one passenger or a load of perishable groceries, crossing Tampa Bay in twenty minutes – hours less than the long way around by auto or train.

In time, tourists drifted away from the old hotels downtown in favor of newer, air-conditioned, year-round resorts on the beach. Downtown languished. The once-elegant Vinoy Hotel was boarded up for years. Other hotels suffered a sorrier fate as seedy flophouses.

Come see the difference a decade has made!

The Vinoy, now an elegant Stouffer hotel, is the perfect place to stay for a sightseeing-packed weekend downtown. Every inch of the hotel has been restored to its former fineness or better, and it has all the amenities demanded by modern travelers: restaurants, lounges, a fitness center, and an inviting pool. Booked here, you're in the center of the newly revitalized downtown, within walking or bicycling distance of many of the best sites.

Even if you don't care for surrealist art, the Salvador Dali Museum is a must. It's not only the largest collection of Dali works in the world, it's a lively activities hub for special exhibits, sizzling fund-raiser parties and balls, education programs, and a superb museum store.

If you're a Dali follower and want to see the museum at your own pace, ask for the brochure describing a self-guided tour. If not, join a group with a docent, who will enrich and enlighten your introduction to a spellbinding artist.

21

Guided tours of the Museum of Fine Arts are also available, or you can browse at your own pace through a noted collection of French impressionist works as well as the largest photography collection in the state.

St. Pete's new (1995) Florida International Museum adds another star to the crown of what is turning into the museum mecca of the state. Its opening exhibit was the world premiere of Treasures of the Czars, the first royal family treasures ever to leave the Kremlin museums in Moscow, and it can be expected that equally stellar events will follow each year.

At press time, the museum has not announced a permanent collection or even whether it expects to have one. Instead, the focus will be on once-in-a-lifetime exhibitions held once each year, usually running for several months. Between times, only the museum shop and perhaps a few other areas will remain open.

During your weekend in downtown St. Petersburg, schedule a day at the Pier with its historical museum, aquarium, restaurants, including one of the Columbias, and shops. Shaped like an inverted pyramid, the five-story landmark is a favorite hangout for locals who gather in its bars and observation deck to watch the sunset.

The Pier and the long, wide approach to it are often filled with special events and festivals that make a popular spot even livelier. The Caribbean Calypso Festival in August is an especially colorful blowout featuring steel bands, limbo dancing, and Caribbean foods including jerk chicken, peas and rice, and fried plantains.

Specifically: St. Petersburg/Clearwater Area Convention and Visitors Bureau, One Stadium Drive, St. Petersburg, FL 33705, 813-582-7892 or 800-345-6710.

9 Horse Around
Ocala

People come to Marion County just to drive up and down country roads gazing at million-dollar horses grazing on green fields surrounded by white fences. It's picture-postcard country, made lively by frolicking colts and proud mares.

While Kentucky is the historic home of thoroughbred horses, much of the industry has moved south because, within an hour of their birth, Florida foals can be gamboling in sunny pastures instead of snuggling with their mothers in cold Kentucky barns. Little legs grow stronger faster.

It all began with a farm called Bonnie Heath, home of Needles, who went on to win the 1956 Kentucky Derby and the Preakness. At least two dozen Ocala-bred horses are in the millionaire category. Precisionist, bred here in 1981, has earned almost $3.5 million, Gate Dancer $2.5 million, Affirmed $2.3 million. The list includes Smile, Cutlass Reality, Tappiano, Carry Back, Island Whirl, and Susan's Girl.

To drive a loop through some of the most scenic horse country, drive west out of town on US 27, north on County 225A, east on 318, then back to Ocala via I-75. The area is laced with country lanes lined with picturebook ranches, so this route is only a starting point. If you want to go farther, you'll need the most recent list of farms and their visitor hours. Call the Florida Thoroughbred Breeders Assocation, 904-629-2160. There is no charge, but it is important to observe hours and rules in hopes that friendly ranchers will continue to maintain an open door policy. Most "tours" are just drive-throughs to take at your own pace in your own vehicle.

Ocala is also home to many other breeds, including miniature horses, Arabians, Appaloosas, palominos, and Mangalarga Marchadors, so check ahead to see what horse shows or other events will be going on during your visit.

Early morning workout near Ocala

If you want to ride, Young's Paso Fino Ranch offers trail rides astride this unusual Spanish breed. Small and silky-maned, paso finos have a unique gait that results in a natural, smooth ride. The ranch also does dinner shows, with country dancing. Call 904-867-5305 to reserve a ride or ask about a tour. If you like equestrian art, furnishings, or souvenirs, visit the Paddock Room Galleries in downtown Ocala, where you'll find the most comprehensive collections this side of Louisville.

Silver Springs, a tourist attraction since the 1890s and now undergoing transition from a commercial attraction to a state park, is worth an entire day. The bird life, aquatic life, pools, river, and forested, natural setting will always be one of Florida's great treasures.

Check into the romantic, ornately gabled Seven Sisters Inn for bed and gourmet breakfast in a Victorian setting. Or stay at the Mediterranean Revival–style Ritz, built in 1925 and now caringly restored. The city also boasts a Hilton and many chain motels. Campers can choose among luxurious RV resorts or several rustic campgrounds in the Ocala National Forest nearby.

While you're in town, visit the Appleton Museum of Art with its excellent collections from a variety of periods. Other attractions include the Don Garlits Museum of Drag Racing, which has more than 100 dragsters and street rods on display, and the collection of some 2,000 antique radios and radio paraphernalia on view at the WMOP studios downtown.

Specifically: Contact the Chamber of Commerce, 110 East Silver Springs Boulevard, Ocala, FL 32678, 352-629-8051. Request lists of accommodations and, just before your visit, the current list of horse farms that welcome visitors.

10 Tartans and Tattoos
Dunedin

It begins in early April with the stirring Tattoo, in which pipers and Scottish dancers from all over the world perform. Among the best are those from Dunedin High School, whose Scottish music and Highland flings hold their own among groups from Canada and even from the mother country itself.

A week later, the Highland Games are played to crowds of up to 40,000 people who come to cheer on athletes as they heave a sixteen-pound sheaf of hay over a bar with a pitchfork. A twenty-foot caber is thrown end over end. A twenty-seven-pound stone is tossed for accuracy and distance. Bagpipers and dancers have their own contests. Food booths sell Scottish favorites, and tartans are seen all over town, even in Flanagan's Hunt Irish Pub.

It's one of Florida's most colorful ethnic festivals, and for a week it transforms this historic hamlet into a Brigadoon. While Greek sponge divers were settling only a few miles to the north, two Scots founded Dunedin in the 1880s, naming it for a city in their homeland. Today, Dunedin is sister city to Stirling, Scotland, and it celebrates its Scottish heritage just as avidly as Tarpon Springs does its Greek traditions.

You can spend the week between the Tattoo and the games on some of the world's best beaches. Caladesi Island can be reached only by boat, but the brief voyage in the Gulf breezes is part of the mystique and romance of a day-long stay here. Most visitors never get beyond the beach, which is a magnificent strand of velvety sand, but the island is also threaded with hiking paths. Nature watching and seashelling here are superb, and the lucky couple may also stumble across the century-old ruins left by the original homesteader. The heartwarming story of this pioneer farm is told by the homesteader's daughter, the late Myrtle Scharrer Betz, in her book *Yesteryear I Lived in Paradise* (sold in Caladesi's gift shop/snack bar).

Unlike Caladesi, neighboring Honeymoon Island can be reached by road, but its beaches too can provide solitude and amour. Once part of Caladesi, Honeymoon became a separate island when a 1920s hurricane drove a channel between them. Before World War II, it was landscaped with palm trees and fragrant vines and developed with rustic, South Seas–style shacks that were sold as honeymoon suites. The enterprise failed, and today both islands are under the protection of the Florida Department of Natural Resources.

If you're baseball fans, keep in mind that Dunedin is also the winter home of the Toronto Blue Jays. By April, when the Highland Games are played, the Toronto team has moved on, but baseball fans can cheer on the Dunedin Blue Jays, a Class A ball club that plays here April through September.

Although Dunedin is a tourist town with a choice of accommodations, one stands out. Every room at the Best Western Jamaica Inn overlooks St. Joseph's Sound from a private balcony or patio. Relaxed, resorty, and very European in style despite its chain affiliation, the inn is co-owned by Munich-born executive chef Karl Heinz Riedl and Peter Werner Kreuziger, who was born in Vienna and educated at Cornell.

Book a bedrooom or efficiency and enjoy surroundings decorated in airy pastels and blond woods to complement grounds abloom with big, yellow flowers. The inn's greatest treasure is its restaurant, Bon Appetit, which has held a four-star Mobil rating for ten years. When asked to name his favorite restaurants, author Dick Francis named Dunedin's Bon Appetit in a list that included New York's Four Seasons and the River Restaurant at the Savoy in London. It's that good.

The inn also operates a yacht, also named *Bon Appetit.*

It's available for charter, complete with captain and chef, for small weddings, or for romantic evenings. If this is the night you're going to propose marriage or celebrate a special anniversary, talk over your plans with Karl and Peter and they'll come up with an enchanted evening choreographed with the sun setting into the Gulf, superb food and wine, and a crew who know when to look the other way.

Specifically: For information about the Highland Games, contact the Chamber of Commerce, 301 Main Street, Dunedin, FL 34698, 813-733-3197. Jamaica Inn reservations, 813-733-4121. Bon Appetit dinner reservations, 813-733-2151.

11 In Love with Anna Maria

The island is as beautiful as its name. A long spit of land that soars out for miles into a silver sea, Anna Maria Island and its twin, Longboat Key, can be reached by road. The long, slow drive through downtown Bradenton can be exasperating, but the reward is a sudden view of the Gulf of Mexico edged with brown-sugar sands.

Shorelines are strung with public beaches, some of them as wide as 200 feet: Coquina Beach, Cortez Beach, Manatee County Beach, and Holmes Beach, all of them studded with the occasional wind-bent palm tree or stand of singing pines. Choose your favorite. Most have picnic areas, restrooms, lifeguards, playgrounds, and snack bars. Cortez Beach and Greer Island, the north end of Longboat Key, have no lifeguards but are ideal for intimate picnics in a grove of casuarinas.

At the north end of Anna Maria, an old wooden pier is a favorite of fishermen. It's also an ideal place to photograph a side view of the Sunshine Skyway Bridge, an engineering marvel that spans Tampa Bay.

Modern history goes back to Hernando De Soto, who landed at the entrance to the Manatee River in 1539. Along a nature trail at the park that now occupies the spot, see native plants that fed and sheltered the Spanish explorers and the Indians before them. De Soto's camp, from which he set out on a four-year expedition in which he reached the Mississippi River, has been restored and is staffed with interpretive characters in sixteenth-century costume.

Downtown, the De Soto Museum has displays and relics from that era, and the South Florida Historical Museum goes into De Soto's story as well as Indian and Civil War history.

Inland on the Manatee River, history buffs are fascinated by Gamble Plantation, the only surviving antebellum mansion in South Florida. It was here that Confederate Secretary of State Judah Benjamin hid in the cane fields to elude pursuing Yankees after the South fell. Tour the home and grounds for the feel of a real-life Tara.

On the opposite side of the river in Bradenton, Manatee Village Historical Park is the home of the first courthouse (1860), an 1889 church, and a 1912 home. Nearby, Castle Park now surrounds the ruins of Braden Castle, a plantation house that is on the National Register of Historic Sites.

Once you've fine-tuned your tan on the beaches, consider taking a sea voyage to remote Egmont Key aboard the *Miss Cortez*. You'll sail out of a ramshackle, century-old fishing village that has a Key West look and feel. Visit the small, free boat building museum, ramble past the docks and fish-packing houses, and pick up a supply of smoked mullet. A Florida specialty, it's delicious when mixed with cream cheese or mayonnaise for use as a canapé spread. Purists simply pick it off the bones with their fingers and eat it in tangy, meaty strips washed down with cold beer.

If you're baseball fans, the Pittsburgh Pirates train in Bradenton in March and April; the Gulf Coast League plays June through August, and the Florida Instructional League plays here in September and October.

The area's best-kept secret is that the Lippizzan stallions are also trained here. Take State 70 east from Bradenton about twenty-five miles to the caution light at Singletary Road, then turn right and go about four miles to the Ottomar Herrmann training grounds. Bring your own lawn chair. Sessions are open to the public only at 3:00 P.M. Fridays and at 10:00 A.M.

on Saturdays, January through March. It's best to call ahead, 813-322-1501 or 813-322-1622.

Specifically: Manatee County Convention and Visitors Bureau, Box 1000, Bradenton, FL 34206. Call 800-4-MANATEE or 813-729-9177.

12 Speed, Speed, Speed
Daytona

Since the dawn of motorcar racing, Daytona Beach has meant high speeds and fast action. In the early days the beaches themselves were the raceways, and the old North Turn Restaurant on the beach is still a popular hangout with drivers and race groupies.

Now well inland, the 2.5-mile and 3.56-mile tracks at Daytona International Speedway are in the world race spotlight throughout the year during the twenty-four-hour race and Daytona 500 in February, the Daytona 200 motorcycle classic in March, and the Pepsi 400 stock car race in July. Many other wheel-related events, including tests, photo shoots, swap meets, and much more, also take place here.

During blockbuster events, the 125,000-seat grandstand spills over with fans from all over the world while hundreds more camp in the infield in tents and RVs. Highways are lined with souvenir hawkers. Favorite hangouts bulge with crowds of drivers, fans, pit crews, international media, and promoters. Heaven help the unwary traveler who gets caught up in the mayhem, because roads clog with traffic, hotels and airline seats are booked months in advance, and there isn't a bar stool to be had at the Hog's Breath Saloon.

What many people don't know is that the Speedway is an exciting destination any day of the year. On days when the track is not in use, tours are available from 9:00 A.M. to 5:00 P.M. Get a close-up look at the 31-degree high banks, the Winston Tower, the pits. Sit through a Surround-Sound presentation that re-creates the rumble of forty racing cars traveling at 190 mph. Linger in the Gallery of Legends and watch film clips of early races on the Video Wall.

Next door to the Speedway, the Klassix Car Museum has an impressive collection of Corvettes and its own ice cream

The flash and roar of the races at Daytona

shop. Friday through Sunday, the Daytona Flea Market near the museum and speedway is one of the largest in the South, with covered walkways and an enclosed antique mall.

Each year in November, Ormond Beach hosts a three-day weekend of antique car meets, a gaslight parade, costumes, parties, street vendors, competitions, and rousing good times.

A regular schedule of Nascar Winston Racing Series events takes place on Friday and Saturday evenings at the Volusia County Speedway, on State 40 in Barberville, which is west of Ormond Beach.

Specifically: Daytona Convention and Visitors Bureau, 126 East Orange Avenue, Daytona Beach, FL 32114, 800-544-0415 or 904-255-0415. Ask about accommodations, race schedules, attractions, and dining. Especially recommended for those who want to avoid the madding crowds are two quiet, family-owned, moderately priced hotels: Perry's Ocean-Edge, where free homemade donuts are served every morning, and the Best Western Aku Tiki, which has a folksy, Polynesian dinner show and popular South Seas dishes. Both are on the World's Most Famous Beach. The historic Live Oak Inn offers fine dining overlooking the showplace marina-restaurant-shopping complex on the mainland side.

13 Discover Bassin'
DeLand

Bob Stonewater raised his family on fish. It's the kind of life most guys only dream about. Bob and his father sold their family iron business in a cold, northern, rust-belt city, and Bob, who had been a business major in college, came south to play for pay.

As a fishing guide out of DeLand on the St. Johns River, he knows where to find lunker bass any day of the year. "Fish have to eat," he says simply. "As long as they have to look for food, I know where to look for them." Whether you're experienced anglers or just want to sample this exciting sport for a weekend, start with a call to Stonewater.

"I'd chartered a lot myself, so I had my own ideas on how to operate a guide service," he says. "My clients don't want to watch me fish. So I let them do it. Some skippers here guarantee that you'll catch a fish, but I'll guarantee fish only if you let me set the hook. And I don't believe the guide should set the hook." As a result, you'll get plenty of hands-on action in the honey holes where Bob knows the big ones are hiding. He's been featured on ESPN and has produced his own bass fishing video.

The historic St. Johns River is in places so narrow and rimmed with jungle growth that it was used for filming the Tarzan movies years ago. In other places, it spreads into major lakes such as Lake George, Lake Monroe, Lake Beresford, and many more. So rich is the bass fishing here that Stonewater once had twenty-eight charters in a row on which at least one six-pounder was caught.

"Some days we get as many as sixty strikes in a day. This is incredible bass country," he says. "When my clients come from up north, where they're used to catching smaller bass, they just can't believe the lunkers that are common here." In his career, he has caught well over 600 ten-pounders.

Stonewater's guests come from Texas, Chicago, St. Louis, the Northeast, Michigan, and even from Alaska and California for the legendary bassing here. Some passionate bassin' fans charter him regularly, to learn bass fishing so they can begin entering high-stakes tournaments. One enthusiastic client came down from Atlanta twice a week for five weeks. He'd never seen such bass.

"Most of my clients come here *just* to fish, so they want more than one day. These are folks who know fishing, and they charter me for two or three days at a time," Stonewater says.

Your weekend could begin by checking into one of the bed and breakfasts in DeLand, a picturesque college town that dates to the last half of the nineteenth-century. Have dinner in the historic, restored downtown. Then choose one of the local coffeehouses for digestifs, poetry, jazz, and mingling with the locals. Daytona's nightspots and beaches are just thirty minutes to the east; downtown Orlando is forty-five minutes to the southwest.

In the morning, meet Bob at a prearranged spot. His speedy, fully equipped bass boat is trailerable, so he can put it in closest to where the fish are biting according to the day's season, weather, river level, and other factors.

"I suggest that my clients buy quality bait, and lots of it. Sometimes a slow day will heat up and suddenly we're going through shiners like crazy. Bass travel a lot, depending on currents, so river fishing is different from lake fishing. Usually, I have six or seven spots picked out that I want to try."

Stonewater can provide tackle, or bring your own favorite rod. "When you're fishing live bait it's important to balance the rod and the bait," he says. "We'll use lures too, especially if the client wants to learn lure fishing for future use in tournaments." He's a concerned conservationist, practices release fishing, and refuses to fish beds during spawning.

Specifically: Bob Stonewater, 179 Glenwood Road, 904-736-7120. DeLand Country Inn Bed and Breakfast, 228 West Howry Avenue, 904-736-4244; the 1888 House Bed and Breakfast, 124 North Clara Avenue, 904-822-4647. DeLand Area Chamber of Commerce, 336 North Woodland Boulevard. All addresses are DeLand 32720.

Other experienced bass fishing guides in the area are Ron and Rick Rawlins, Highland Park Fish Camp, 904-734-2334.

14 Movie Mania
Orlando

When MGM-Disney Studios opened at Walt Disney World, movie buffs thronged here to hang out at Hollywood and Vine, dine at the Brown Derby, and shop for authentic memorabilia signed by such movie legends as Joan Crawford and Clark Gable. Then came Universal Studios, Nickelodeon Studios, and multiple sound stages in almost nonstop production for movies and television, and thrilled fans found that Orlando had become a major star in the filmmaking galaxy.

How about spending a fantasy weekend at, in, around, and behind the scenes at the movies?

Generations ago, Florida had its first chance at becoming the cinema capital of the nation. New York, the big apple for artists and actors, was a natural spot for the movie industry to take root. In winter, when weather was a problem, productions could be moved easily to Jacksonville, which was only an overnight train ride away. Dozens of early flicks were shot there. Still, the iffy winters of north Florida were no match for the bright, dry climate of southern California. By the 1920s most of the industry had moved west.

Today it's back in Florida. Don't ask whether the MGM-Disney or the Universal Studios park is better. Just *go*, reserving at least one full day and evening for each—longer if you want to see it all.

The parks really have two purposes. The most obvious one is to attract visitors with their rides and shows, shops, dining, street performers, and realistic movie-set ambiance: New York, the New England village where Jaws lurks just offshore, San Francisco, Grauman's Chinese Theater, Mel's Diner, and dozens more street sets. You can spend an entire weekend in delicious make-believe.

Second, but perhaps more important to the studios' bottom line, is the actual production, day and night, of television shows, movies, and commercials. Many productions in the making are open for audience viewing or even audience participation; others are being filmed in cordoned-off sections of the parks. Keep an eye peeled for cameras, stars, and surprises. You can leave the world of nostalgic fantasy any time and plug into the frenzied zing of real-life moviemaking.

Florida insiders often taken advantage of free studio filmings, which do not require theme park admission. Write ahead to your favorite shows, following instructions on how to get free tickets (they're usually broadcast at the end of each show). Or ask the concierge at your hotel to get current taping schedules.

No matter what aspect of the parks you want to zero in on, you're assured of excellence. Rides and shows such as Jaws, Kongfrontation, Twilight Zone, Tower of Terror, and the Great Movie Ride are so spectacular you may want to go through them more than once. Meals can be quick and quirky or long and elegant. At Disney's Prime Time Cafe, waitresses play Mom and coax you to eat your meatloaf and mashed potatoes while you watch black-and-white reruns of "I Love Lucy." For dinner at the great Brown Derby, reservations are recommended.

At Universal Studios, dine on seafood at the Cafe Alcatraz, sip a soda at Schwab's Pharmacy, eat Italian at Louie's, or slip out to the guitar-shaped Hard Rock Cafe. It's accessible from within the theme park or from outside.

Both parks are filled with surprises. Suddenly a fracas breaks out between a "cop" and a "cabbie" who has illegally parked his 1940s Checker. Or you're approached by a director who insists that you rush over to Make-Up. Or Louella

Kongfrontation at Universal Studios

Parsons asks you for a scoop. Or Ricky and Lucy break into a shtick on the street.

Music, parades, and shows, both scheduled and seemingly extemporaneous, pop up constantly. Shops offer collectibles, souvenirs, logo clothing, and unique treasures. Both parks have quiet greens where you can sit in the cool shade, watch the passing scene, and pretend that you're in Tinsel Town, circa 1940, waiting to be discovered.

It takes more than one day, even more than one visit, to catch the rhythm of movie mania. Make your first visit one of orientation and discovery; your second a time to linger in whatever layer of Hollywood, past or present, serves up the romantic weekend that is right for the two of you.

Specifically: See your travel agent about packages that include theme park admissions and accommodations at Walt Disney World, where thousands of hotel rooms are available in more than a dozen resorts. Universal Studios is adding resort facilities, including four hotels that will begin opening in 1997.

15 Sample a Club Med Evening

Pssst. Want to spend a flashy evening at one of those racy resorts, have a fabulous French meal, and see a spectacular show?

Club Med Sandpiper at Port St. Lucie, near Stuart, has long been one of the state's zippiest, most switched-on resorts. It is also one of the few Club Meds in the world that accepts reservations for the evening. Here, you can be a part of the fabulous, frenzied Club Med without committing to an expensive week-long package. Try it for one evening before deciding if the Club Med scene is for you.

On the plus side, Club Meds offer a clubby sense of belonging. Guests pay yearly dues that entitle them to visit exotic Club Meds all over the world. Rates are high, but once you arrive you can forget your wallet. Only bar drinks are extra.

You can expect lavish meals, beer and wine with lunch and dinner, a long list of sports, including golf and sailing, archery lessons, tennis instruction, and oodles of extras. On the minus side, your fellow guests may arrive by the planeload in huge, hungry, pushy packs. It's not for everyone.

Club Med, the resort chain that started in France and spread all over the world from Mexico to Morocco, is still thought of by many people as a hotbed of hanky-panky. Yet local custom is respected, which means that bathing suits, both top and bottom, are very much a part of the scene at the Club Med Sandpiper. Club Meds are not just for swinging singles, nudies, jocks, or hellraisers. In an evening that includes dinner, a Las Vegas–style show, and disco until 2:00 A.M., you won't see anything that is not rated PG.

Before dinner, gather around the bar, where professional entertainers are usually on hand to organize a mixer or a game. Or join a quiet group on the porch overlooking the St. Lucie River to sip a sundowner while you listen to a recorded concert of classical music. Five minutes into the evening, you belong. Other guests are a mix of French, Canadians, Americans, Belgians, Germans, and Japanese, but there are no strangers. Even though everything is said in both French and English, you understand it all.

When dinner is announced at 7:30 sharp, file in and you'll be seated at a table for eight. You may be placed with a couple newly arrived from France, a supermarket manager from New Jersey, two career girls in search of a man and a tan, or a middle-aged couple who vacation at a different Club Med every year.

At each table are one or two G.O.'s.—that stands for gentle organizers, who are Club Med employees. Your table partner could be a waterski instructor, the bookkeeper, the swim shop clerk, or the star of tonight's show. It's fun to talk to the G.O.'s about their footloose, singles lifestyle. They spend no more than six months at each club, so most of them have been all over the Club Med world.

Guests are called G.M.'s, or gentle members (*gentils membres* if you *parlez français*). As a dinner guest, you're not quite a G.M., but never mind. The idea is to mix everyone up family-style, and that's part of the fun.

Dinner is a culinary event because the French wouldn't have it any other way. There are entire tables of salad makings, far more elegant than any salad bar. One chef does nothing but serve cheese, more flavors than most Americans ever heard of. One table is filled with luscious, freshly baked French breads.

Start with soup and a hot appetizer that could be an omelet, fresh fish, or quiche. Pace yourself. There's more. After these opening courses, with as much of any wine as you care to have, waiters bring on the main course. It could be fairly conventional meat-potato dishes or your choice of some exotic, gustatory adventure.

The wine keeps flowing, then comes dessert, then coffee. You end your meal in French style with fruit and cheese. The show, performed by the G.O.'s you met earlier working the front desk or waiting tables in the restaurant, is snazzy and professional. Costumes are lavish, staging and lighting first rate, and the enthusiasm is unbounded.

The bar stays open and the good times roll in the disco until 2:00 A.M. Don't be shy about mixing, dancing, and being part of the fun. This is, remember, a club. There's only one problem. How ya gonna keep 'em down on the farm after they've seen Paree?

Specifically: Club Med Sandpiper, 3500 S.E. Morningside Boulevard, Port St. Lucie, FL 34952. For evening reservations at Club Med Sandpiper, call 407-335-4400, ext. 6612. If you arrive by boat, dockage during dinner is free. Or pay dockage and stay overnight. Marina reservations, ext. 6614. Accommodations in the area include the beachfront Indian River Plantation Resort, 555 N.E. Ocean Boulevard, Hutchinson Island, FL 34996, 407-225-3700 or 800-444-3389.

16 A Ridin', Ropin' Rodeo Weekend
Kissimmee

By the time it comes to the table, Florida beef has been fattened elsewhere, so most people don't realize that the Sunshine State is a major cattle producer. Kissimmee, in the heart of cattle country, is the home of the fifty-year-old Silver Spurs Rodeo, one of the most exciting and important rodeos in North America. Nearby is a living-history Cow Camp peopled by role-playing cow hunters tending rare scrub cattle and true marshtackie horses.

Cattle raising here began with the first Spanish settlers, who brought in specially bred cattle to survive in the hot, swampy bush. They also introduced the sturdy, sure-footed marshtackie horses that cowpokes relied on to hunt scrub cattle in the almost impenetrable wilderness.

The kind of ropings, round-ups, and stampedes made famous in western movies wouldn't work in Florida. Cow hunters (the term "boy" was resented) relied on their cowhide whips instead of lassos to "pop" cattle out of the scrub. The beeves were so important a food source to the Confederacy that Florida cow hunters were exempt from the draft. After the war, fortunes were made in cattle that were loaded onto boats, shipped to Havana, and paid for in Spanish gold.

Silver Spurs rodeos, held in Kissimmee every February and July, star professional, world-class cowboys in traditional bronc riding, steer wrestling, and barrel racing events. Order tickets weeks in advance. Visitors can also get a look at the local cattle market at weekly auctions held in Kissimmee. Don't miss the barbecue that is held at the end of each auction day.

Open on weekends at Lake Kissimmee State Park, the Cow Camp re-creates the look and feel of the open range in the 1870s. Park rangers serve as cow hunters, answering all

Whooping it up at the rodeo in Kissimmee

your questions as long as they don't involve anything that happened in modern times. Keep in mind that Ulysses S. Grant is president and that a square meal costs two bits. The cow hunter probably can't read, and couldn't get his hands on a newspaper anyway. His life is to "pop" cattle and pen them until it's time to drive them to Punta Rassa (near the present-day city of Fort Myers). If he doesn't die with yellow jack, or get rattlesnake-bit, he might live to be an old man of sixty.

In this quiet, backwoods camp, scrub cattle doze in the sun in their split-rail corral, flicking their tails at hovering flies. A marshtackie horse rummages around in its water bucket. A smoky fire keeps a coffeepot at a slow simmer outside a thatched hut. A cow hunter coils his whip and keeps it on his hip. "It cracks, so they calls us Crackers," he explains. "Some of the men can snap the head offen a rattlesnake with a whip. Me, I uses it to catch marsh rabbits and squirrels. Eat the beef? No siree. We sells it for Spanish gold."

Life in camp is not fancy. At night there's a wood bunk with a rope spring and a wool army blanket, with nothing but a woven palm roof to keep out the rain and nothing at all to keep out the mosquitoes. Malaria is a problem; yellow fever is deadly. These simple men never knew any other life.

Still, the camaraderie is good, and the pay includes grub. There's usually plenty of grits, cornmeal, bacon, and coffee, sometimes wheat flour for biscuits, and all the game you can find. Wild boar are delicious, and good riddance when one is hunted down because their rooting leaves potholes that can break a cow's leg. The nearest civilization is at Bartow Town, where a man can have a good whip made for a dollar a foot. A dollar. That's a day's pay.

Specifically: Lake Kissimmee State Park, 14248 Camp Mack Road, Lake Wales, FL 33853, 813-696-1112. The Cow

Camp operates on weekends and some holidays, 8:30 A.M. to 4:30 P.M. The state park also has campsites, fishing, boating, picnicking, and nature trails. For information on Silver Spurs rodeos, held in February and July, call 407-67-RODEO. For Kissimmee information, call 800-831-1844 or 407-847-5000. Kissimmee hotel reservations, 800-333-KISS.

17 A Fairytale Wedding
Walt Disney World

If this is the weekend when the two of you will make or renew your vows, the Imagineers at Walt Disney World can make it a dream come true, and then some. Picture yourselves leaving the ceremony in Cinderella's coach, drawn by horses and driven by uniformed footmen. Or acting out an Aladdin fantasy. Or having Mickey and Minnie Mouse in your receiving line. Or having dinner à deux in the intimacy of Victoria and Albert's at the sumptuous Grand Floridian resort.

The most popular honeymoon destination in the nation, WDW is also a winning site for weddings, anniversaries, vow renewal celebrations, and other special events. Weddings can take place at such WDW resorts as the Grand Floridian, Yacht Club and Beach Club, Contemporary Resort, Disney's Village Resort, or aboard the *Empress Lily* riverboat.

Talented wedding coordinators on the Disney staff can arrange everything from rented tuxes to flowers, music, invitations, food, accommodations for all the wedding guests, a honeymoon suite, the rehearsal dinner, and even beauty shop and barber appointments for both of you, all within Walt Disney World.

Although many couples choose a theme tied to a favorite Disney character or movie, many others select more traditional ceremonies under an arbor of roses or overlooking a lake. Describe your dream. Chances are they can make it come true, complete with magic and pixie dust.

Best of all, it's in a world of its own in which you have an enormous choice of hotels, restaurants, private reception rooms, lounges with music and dancing, theme parks, golf, swimming pools, tennis courts, boating, nature walks, horseback riding, canoeing through a nature preserve, bicycling and much more, all of it accessed by WDW's free transportation system. Nobody has to worry about cars and parking.

If you haven't been to WDW lately, you're in for a surprise. More than 20,000 rooms are available among a dozen resorts, each with its own theme and personality. Rates range from moderate at the Caribbean Beach, Dixie Landings, and Port Orleans to the stunning Grand Floridian, where you'll find the utmost in hotel luxury in the fifteen honeymoon suites. This grandly Edwardian hotel is a complete resort in itself. Order from room service or choose among six restaurants. Grandest of them all and one of the finest restaurants in Orlando is the tiny (sixty-eight-seat) Victoria and Albert's. Prices are high; the dress code requires jackets; reservations are essential.

You'll be served continental cuisine on Royal Doulton china, will eat with Sambonet silver, and drink from the most delicate crystal. Although the wine list is comprehensive, menu choices are limited because the chef personally supervises the shopping, choosing only the finest, freshest ingredients each day. You'll leave with a hand-written souvenir menu, a red rose, and memories of a meal worthy of this once-in-a-lifetime weekend.

During your stay you might also visit the hotel's 1900 Park Fare, a buffet restaurant with a 100-year-old band organ, and Flagler's, an Italian restaurant overlooking the marina. Southern cooking is served at the Grand Floridian Cafe, and burgers and pizza reign at the Gasparilla Grill.

Rent a boat or swim in the enormous pool. Bask on white sand at the lagoon. The resort has its own tennis courts, a fitness club for the exclusive use of Grand Floridian guests, croquet and volleyball. All other features throughout WDW, such as golf or theme park tickets, can, of course, be arranged by the concierge.

The Grand Floridian has its own lounges, but for zestier nightlife there is nothing quite like Pleasure Island. It's a complete theme park for adults, with separate clubs offering jazz, rock 'n' roll, comedy, country and western, and the wonderfully wacky Adventurers Club. Every night is New Year's Eve with a street party and fireworks. Dine at one of the fine restaurants, or snack and shop your way around the various eateries, pubs, specialty shops, and cozy hideaways. Admission to shops and restaurants is free until 7:00 P.M. After that, one ticket buys all the clubs and entertainment until about 2:00 A.M.

Specifically: Call 407-363-6333 for information about a Disney wedding or vow-renewal ceremony. For central reservations, call 407-W-DISNEY. For a complete guide to the worlds of Disney read Birnbaum's *Walt Disney World,* the Official Guide (Hyperion and Hearst Business Publishing). It is thoroughly revised every year.

18 Harvest Nature's Plenty

If sweaty stoop labor isn't your idea of a romantic weekend, picture a field of plump strawberries ripe for the picking or acres of bushes bending with the weight of bursting-ripe blueberries. There's something earthy and satisfying about honest farm work and the timeless joy of the gathering in. To a modern couple who spend their working hours at desks, a weekend in the fields can be energizing and surprisingly erotic.

All the other weekends in this book come in various price ranges from budget to splurge. This one is on the profit side of the ledger. With a day's easy, pleasant work in the sun and air, you can come home with enough fresh produce to make preserves and pies for the rest of the year. Or if you're too far from home, simply stuff yourselves silly as you pick and take enough back to your motel to keep yourself in breakfast for the rest of your stay.

Begin by writing for the U-Gather Directory. It's updated periodically as farms are added and deleted. Although it's common to stumble on u-pick farms all over the state, it's best to plan this weekend as carefully as any other. Contact the farmer ahead of time for information on when the crop will be ripe and for exact directions on how to find the field.

Don't confuse u-picking with gleaning, in which people are let into harvested fields to help themselves to leftovers at little or no cost. These gardens offer top-quality produce in its prime. Costs are less than supermarket prices, and you are getting the pick of the crop at the peak of freshness, but it isn't a giveaway.

Think about scuppernong, or muscadine, grapes, swollen with juice for making your own jelly or wine. And peaches sticky with sweetness. And velvety persimmons ripened to perfection. On evergreen farms, you can choose your own Christmas tree. Other farms, for a fee, let you fill your creel with catfish you land yourself.

Farms that have only one crop, such as strawberries or peaches, may be open only a few weeks each season or, as one blueberry farmer reports, "June until gone." The farther north you go in the state, the more intense the harvest over a shorter period. Florida offers an enormous variety of seasons and produce.

Dress for the weather and be prepared for rain. No matter how lightly you dress in hot weather, however, it's important to wear substantial shoes or boots and a hat to shade you from the sun. If possible, wear long sleeves and trousers to protect against burrs and brambles. Wear bug spray and, where advisable, a tick repellent. Most u-pick fields are as well groomed as a park, but some can be buggy, boggy, or overgrown.

Take enough food and water for the day because you may be miles from the nearest restaurant. Ask farmers if you should bring your own containers. They may provide containers for the picking and measuring, after which you must transfer the produce to baskets or cartons you provide.

Here is a sampling of the state's u-pick crops:

Apples, blueberries, cantaloupes, u-fish catfish, u-cut or potted Christmas trees, grapes, persimmons, peaches, strawberries, and miscellaneous crops, including tomatoes, potatoes, squash, collards, turnips, cauliflower, watermelon, black-eyed or purple hull peas, cucumbers, green beans, speckled butter beans, onions, cabbage, peppers, okra, sweet corn, and eggplant. Some farms specialize in organic farming or Oriental vegetables.

Specifically: Bureau of Market Development, Florida Department of Agriculture, 426 Mayo Building, Tallahassee, FL 32399. Fax, 904-488-7127, telephone, 904-488-9682. Ask for the U-Gather Directory.

19 Make a Splash in a Water Park

In summer Floridians not only beat the heat, they look forward to it as the time to immerse themselves, literally, in some of the best water parks in the world. Climbing temperatures mean happy, splashy, exciting days in high-tech rides, slides, artificial coamers, fountains, and mountains. Make a weekend out of "collecting" the best of Florida's water parks.

Walt Disney World's razzle-dazzle water parks include Blizzard Beach, with a theme of snow-covered mountains, and Typhoon Lagoon where seven-foot coamers are actually high enough for real surfing. The Lagoon has its own saltwater reef where the adventurous can snorkel among real fish, and a mile-long lazy river to float in a tube. Mickey, Minnie, Donald, Pluto, and the rest of the Disney gang are there, having fun with you in all the chutes, challenges, thrills, and dousings of first-class water parks.

Only a few years ago, most water parks had only a few zingy slides, some artificial waves, a kiddy pool, and one or two kamakazis for older kids. Today, the sky's the limit. The old wave pool may still be there, but many parks now have waves that are high and powerful enough to ride on surfboards. The two of you can share high adventure on shrieking thrill rides, float a lazy river, then sun the day away on a white sand "beach."

A typical menu is that at Adventure Island, a Busch Gardens project in Tampa. Try the triple-tube waterslide, ride a rambling bayou float stream, then dare a free-fall body slide that sends you hurtling down 76 feet, a 210-foot speed slide, a 72-foot sled slide, and a 450-foot inner descent by inner tube. The 9,000-square-foot swimming pool is fed by cascading waterfalls.

Florida has water parks all over the state, from Shipwreck

Island in Panama City Beach to Ski Rixen, a "boatless" water-ski attraction in Pompano Beach, and Wild Waters, a six-acre water park adjoining Silver Springs. At Weeki Wachee, get a combination ticket that includes the mermaid show and other exhibits at the springs plus a cool-down in Buccaneer Bay. You'll swim in a spring-fed river, ride the flumes, and sun on a natural river sand beach. It's probably the only water park in the nation that runs on spring water.

In addition to Blizzard Beach and Typhoon Lagoon, Walt Disney World offers River Country, a water park based on a rustic, lazy, swimmin' hole theme. Even the hotel pools at WDW are special in some way, each with its own fountains, waterfalls, grottos, and other surprises. One even has a sand bottom.

Wet 'n Wild has to be spectacular to compete in Orlando's action-packed attractions area. Ride the Surge, the longest, fastest, multipassenger ride in the Southeast. It is 600 feet of swirling, twirling, soaking fun in a park filled with rides, slides, and spectacular water attractions.

Nearby in Kissimmee, Water Mania offers fourteen thrilling rides, from the screaming Wipe Out to the relaxing float down Cruisin' Creek. The picnic area alone covers three acres.

Specifically: For a list of water parks, write the World Waterpark Association, P.O. Box 14826, Lenaxa, KS 66214 or request the Florida Vacation Guide from Florida Tourism, 126 Van Buren Street, Tallahassee, FL 32399. It lists water parks with other attractions for each region. Always call ahead. Some Florida water parks are closed seasonally; others change their hours to suit the season. Ask too about rules. Some parks offer a picnic area; others prohibit coolers and other personal gear.

20 A Summer at Seaside

It appears at first to be a Victorian community frozen in time, but Seaside was actually built in the 1980s according to a precise, utopian plan that is setting the model for new communities all over the world. Designed around a village green with a grid of streets that invites walking and bicycling rather than driving, the village fronts on one of the fabled beaches of Florida's Panhandle.

Florida beaches could fill an entire book with superlatives about rocky blowholes, brown-sugar sands, and seashell-strewn shores. The beaches of the Panhandle, however, are unique. Grains of silica sand, ground to impossible fineness in the tumbling Gulf, are as white as fresh snow against the deep neon green of the water.

On the minus side is a four-season climate that can send temperatures toppling into the teens during winter cold fronts. Come in high season, May through October, to relive carefree summertimes when gentlemen in straw boaters called on ladies in starched lawn gowns to spend thoughtful evenings in the gazebo.

Even the entertainments of Seaside stray into yesteryear. Like the chautauquas of Northeastern resorts at the turn of the century, Seaside has a comprehensive schedule of theater, readings, seminars, and tastings.

The hamlet has its own bed and breakfast, Josephine's, where dinner is also available by reservation. Each unit in the main house has a private bath, wet bar, microwave, and coffeemaker. In the guest house are two one-bedroom suites with full kitchen and living/dining area. Everywhere the amenities of times gone by have been faithfully incorporated: claw-foot bathtubs, wainscoting, heart-pine flooring, Battenburg comforters on four-poster beds, and fireplaces.

Dozens of homes throughout the community are available for rent by the week or month. Find your favorite or try them all. All have kitchens, at least one bathroom, and artful furnishings.

Although some accommodations appeal more to families who need to bunk as many as twelve or fifteen people, couples in search of a quiet hideaway can find sweet little cottages such as the Picture Book, which has one room and a sleeping loft, the one-bedroom Romance, which is reached by a path between the picket fences, or the Benedictus, a dollhouse with balconies overlooking the Gulf.

Upstairs over the Ruskin Place Artist Colony, the one-bedroom Maiden's Chamber has a forty-foot balcony, complete with a kitchen, an outdoor grill, and a hammock on the deck. Marietta's Cottage, surrounded by climbing roses, has a spiral staircase to the single bedroom.

Basic supplies and services (rental car, post office), upscale shops, and dining and snacking are available in Seaside. For major provisioning at supermarket prices, Destin is thirty minutes to the west and Panama City is fifty minutes to the east.

Come here to discover the sea, each other, and perhaps a new way of life.

Specifically: Contact Monarch Realty, Box 786, Tallahassee, FL 32302, 904-561-0686 or 800-848-1841, for information about cottages. Josephine's Bed and Breakfast Inn, Box 786, Tallahassee, FL 32302, 904-561-0566 or 800-848-1840.

21 A Waterskiing Weekend

The sport was invented in Minnesota, but today the center of the waterskiing world is Winter Haven, Florida. It is here that champions come to teach, where contenders come to train, and where the best performers come to star in the famous waterskiing shows at Cypress Gardens.

No matter what your level of waterskiing skills, an exciting and challenging weekend in central Florida will bring you closer to the world of sport and to each other. Most heart-warming of all, waterskiing is one of the few sports that can be shared by all couples of all ages and all physical abilities or disabilities.

Ann O'Brine, a paraplegic who has been the women's world champion sit skiier, trains and teaches here. So does Geoff Brown, an Irish athlete who was injured in Australia and wound up paraplegic. He came to Florida, took up sit skiing, and promptly wheeled away with silver and bronze medals in a Cypress Gardens Open. Write ahead for information on the schools in the area, then choose one that is right for you both. No longer just one sport, waterskiing is a multifaceted activity in which you'll move on from basic training into barefoot skiing, swivel, slalom, kneeboarding, tricks, jumping, or advanced skiing for fun or competition. Once you start on the addictive road to competition, the sky is the limit.

Contests are held throughout the world, so you might start competing in your hometown and let your love for waterskiing take you around the world. Skiing embraces a huge family with a place at the meet for everyone, male and female, adult, elderly, youths, children, and people who are deaf, blind, paralyzed, or minus a limb or two, with or without prostheses.

Although many people learn waterskiing in a hometown lake with the help of friends, it's best to get off on the right foot with correct training, equipment, safety habits, and a suitable boat with a ski-savvy driver. A general school will be best if one of you is just starting out and the other is advanced. If you're both ready to progress to barefoot or trick skiing, select one of the specialty schools. If one or both of you require a ski school and accommodations with wheelchair access, Lake Roy is accessible and so is its shoreside motel.

Two romantic bed and breakfasts are found nearby. Chalet Suzanne in Lake Wales has been famous since the 1930s for its superb cuisine and wine cellar. Its accommodations are uniquely skewed and zany, set in a European village filled with flowers. Ask about packages that include breakfast and dinner. J.D.'s Southern Oaks is a bed and breakfast in a lovingly restored old mansion.

While you're in town, take time to stroll through the winding pathways of Cypress Gardens. Ride a silent electric boat cruise through dark cypress swamps that are bright with one of the earth's greatest flower shows. See the new butterfly conservatory, view shows such as the breathtaking waterskiing extravaganza, ride the Island in the Sky, and pause at every photo spot to take snapshots of each other with the waterfalls, blossoms, topiaries, and flowering shrubs. Winter Haven is also the home of the Water Ski Hall of Fame, so save an hour to see it too.

Specifically: Write the American Water Ski Association, 799 Overlook Drive, S.E., Winter Haven, FL 33884, for a list of local-area ski schools. Lake Roy Motor Lodge, 813-324-7894, has rooms and efficiencies, including accessible units. Chalet Suzanne, P.O. Drawer AC, Lake Wales, FL 33859; 813-676-6011 or 800-288-6011. J.D.'s Southern Oaks, 3800 Country Club Road, Winter Haven, FL 33881, 813-293-2335.

22 Canoe the True Florida

Picture cold, clear water, so clean you could drink it, tunneling through a matted tangle of primeval jungle. The day is cool and moist. The air is alive with birdcalls and buzzing insects. Your canoe slips through the water, silent as a kiss.

Picture rivers that run almost to the edge of skyscraper-filled cities yet the silence is so serene that sunning turtles are startled at your stealthy approach. Picture springs that start with a mere oozing from the earth and swell into sparkling streamlets that pour into great rivers.

Florida can't provide the crashing, whitewater thrills found in other states. Yet canoeing here is dramatic and exciting in its own way, offering a rich and natural sharing that a couple will remember and cherish for years ever after.

The scene can be deceptively tame. Waters flow at walking speed, requiring little more than paddle power to maneuver around a fallen tree here or a sandbar there. Stop here to fish, there to spread a picnic lunch or sunbathe on a snow white sandbar and await the quiet dramas that are played out around you.

Dramas? Judge for yourself. You're rounding a bend in a spring run that's barely wider than the canoe, and you come face to face with a twelve-foot alligator sunning on a log. You drop something overboard and have to paddle wildly against the current to try to retrieve it.

A giant tree has fallen across the creek, closing it. Lying in the bottom of the canoe to squeeze under it, you look up to see a harmless, but brilliantly beautiful, green tree snake staring down at you.

A raccoon looks up as you pass and pauses in his diligent laundering of the tree oyster he's about to eat. Along a forgotten river, a monkey scolds at your intrusion. You blink unbelievingly, then remember that colonies of monkeys escaped during the filming of Tarzan movies in Florida in the 1930s and '40s. They've continued to breed in the wild.

Cypress knees loom out of the water, and Spanish moss droops from overhanging trees in a Louisiana Bayou movie set. In the endless water mazes that make up the Everglades, paddle past island rookeries that are so covered with birds you can hardly see the trees. Look more closely at a floating raft of sticks and see the eggs left there by a nesting sandhill crane.

Explore the hidden reaches of the upper St. Johns River, where wild boar root along the banks and showy marsh-mallow blooms on boggy islands. Try to outpaddle a vee of coots or the mother duck with her trailing brood. They'll run rings around you.

Among the best canoeing waters in Florida are the Suwannee, Alapaha, northern and southern Withlacoochee, Sante Fe, Ichetucknee, Wekiwa, Hillsborough, Little Manatee, and Peace rivers, the Everglades, and the spring runs in the Ocala National Forest. Outfitters along these waterways provide canoes and other equipment, drop-off/pickup, and camping equipment rental in areas where overnight trips are practical. The Ichetucknee is also popular with floaters who rent inner tubes for the fanny-freezing, three-hour float.

Before you go, learn as much as possible about local nature sightings, hazards, and rules. No food or drink is permitted on some pristine waters. On others, you can pack in supplies to camp and explore for days. Try to avoid large lakes and rivers where motorboat traffic can be a problem.

Specifically: Write Florida Tourism, 107 West Gaines Street, Tallahassee, FL 32399, and ask for a list of canoe rental outlets or check local Yellow Pages under Boat Rentals. Many state parks and other agencies also offer ranger-led canoe expeditions for small groups and on limited schedules. Learn about them through newspapers or local tourism information kiosks.

In addition to an extensive network of canoe waters and outfitters, sea kayaking is becoming very popular in Florida. Your hotel or resort may offer kayaks for rent, or find rentals through the Yellow Pages. Adventure travelers take note: Florida Adventures, Inc., Box 677923, Orlando, FL 32867, 407-677-0655, is a central booking agency for active Florida travels statewide, including day and overnight canoe trips.

23 Summer's Isle
Amelia Island

One of Florida's best-kept secrets is that Georgia's Golden Isles, wave-swept and aglow, straggle across the state line into the Sunshine State. Amelia Island offers an enchanted weekend in almost any packaging you choose: active sports such as tennis or sailing, lazing at the beach with a good book, horseback riding through the surf, pub crawling in the funky village of Fernandina Beach, or playing some of the state's most vaunted golf courses, including a true Scottish-style links.

It's the perfect destination for an unhurried driving weekend out of Atlanta or Orlando; if you fly in from New York (1.5 hours) or London (8 hours), the island is only twenty-five minutes from Jacksonville International. Yet it's so aloof, tucked into a niche that nudges into Georgia, that most visitors speed past the exit on I-95 and never know this treasure exists.

The name is credited to James Oglethorpe, founder of Savannah, whose Scottish regiments once occupied the headlands here. He named the island for Amelia, an English princess, and ever since it has been steeped in romance and intrigue.

For almost two centuries, the island was yanked back and forth between Spanish, English, and other powers so often it has served under eight flags. Through it all, Amelia stayed a sort of buffer zone that always muddled through. American ports were closed to foreign shipping in 1807, so Caribbean pirates flowed into Fernandina, which was still Spanish. The United States banned further importing of African slaves, but slave ships could come here because Florida was not yet a state. Even during Prohibition, Jacksonville's thirsty could find a friendly rumrunner or moonshiner somewhere on Amelia Island.

The island, which is only thirteen miles long and two miles wide, spreads from the tangled live oak forests at its south end to Fernandina Beach with street after street of Victorian mansions, to the beachfront campground in Fort Clinch State Park. Start your weekend of discovery at Centre Street with its shops and restaurants, all of them historic buildings that have been lovingly restored. The Palace Saloon is Florida's oldest saloon operating on the same site. Locals and tourists hang out here, drinking suds and eating steamed shrimp or popcorn.

A good choice of upscale restaurants is available in town. The 1878 Steak House cuts, cooks, and sauces steaks to order. Or order seafood fresh from the local fleet. Boardinghouse-style home cooking is the specialty at the Florida House. Chef Michael's on Centre Street serves continental cuisine, and The Marina across from the old railroad depot (now the Chamber of Commerce) is a sunny favorite overlooking the water.

Stop at the Book Loft at 214 Centre Street to buy a guidebook to the town and start your walking tour downtown with its stately courthouse and antique post office. Then walk, bicycle, or drive up one side street and down the next starting at North Third. Particularly good Victorian neighborhoods are found on South Seventh and North Sixth, but it's best to follow the booklet block by block.

After rubbernecking the Victorian neighborhoods, drive north on Fourteenth Street and stop at Bosque Bello Cemetery. Its older sections tell an eloquent story of the island's waves of immigration, its yellow fever epidemics, and the loss of sailors at sea. Continue north, then turn left on White

Street to the waterfront plateau the Spanish called Plaza San Marcos.

Today it's just an open field overlooking the river and salt marshes, but good historical markers tell the story of its history from 2000 B.C. through the English occupation. Much of the original land has been eroded away, but you may want to photograph the one fine Victorian home that still overlooks the site. There are no facilities, but it's a quiet spot to spread a blanket and a picnic lunch.

Fort Clinch State Park, surrounded by water, covers the northeast point of the island. The brick fort, built in 1847,

A walk along the beach may turn up some treasures

was used only briefly in the Civil War and the War of 1812. Now its 1,000 plus acres are a playground: beaches and oak forest, campsites, fishing in the marshes or ocean, a fishing pier, bird-watching, picnic tables, and nature paths.

Perhaps best known for its authentically Scottish ocean-side links designed by Pete Dye, Amelia Island Plantation also has a total of forty-five holes of golf plus tennis courts known for the big-name tournaments played here. Both the Plantation and the Ritz-Carlton are plush resorts with all the bells and whistles. The island also offers almost a dozen bed and breakfasts, the state's oldest hotel (the Florida House Inn), oceanside or forest campsites, and a selection of private rentals.

Specifically: Chamber of Commerce, 102 Centre Street, Fernandina Beach, FL 32034, 904-261-3248.

24 The Emerald Coast
Pensacola

Geographically more a part of Alabama and Georgia than Florida, this part of the Panhandle is less charmingly called the Redneck Riviera. Yet Pensacola has a swashbuckling past, a jet-age present thanks to naval aviation, incredibly white beaches that crunch underfoot like fresh-fallen snow, and a nice mix of people of all ages. The old cornpone label doesn't fit anymore.

Technically, Pensacola and not St. Augustine should be called America's first city. It was settled before St. Augustine but was abandoned and resettled later. The Seville Historic District, which includes the area known as Pensacola Village, is the historic heart of the old city, filled with museums, Old Christ Church, a cemetery that makes for pleasant and pensive strolling, and a host of historic homes.

In the North Hill Preservation District, one of three major historic neighborhoods, Victorian homes built by early lumber barons maintain an almost perfect time warp. The district covers fifty blocks, a treasury of American architecture from 1870 to 1930.

The Palafox District with its iron lace balconies includes the lavishly restored Saenger Theater, the once-elegant San Carlos Hotel, and the T. T. Wentworth Florida State Museum. It's the area just north of Palafox Pier. Stroll the old streets, stop at sidewalk cafés, and soak up centuries of history as you study homes in the Folk Victorian, Frame Vernacular, and Creole Homestead styles.

Quayside is the largest cooperative art gallery in the South. Quayside Market is pleasantly packed with antique sellers in nooks and crannies. Wall South is the nation's first full-name replica of the Vietnam Veterans Memorial in

Washington, D.C. Seville Quarter is a lusty entertainment complex much like Church Street Station in Orlando.

The area's old forts range from mere fragments in the center of the city to massive Fort Pickens, which is faced across the bay by Fort Barrancas. The two, planned as pincers to snare any enemy ship that dared to invade the bay, became enemies themselves when one was occupied by the Confederacy, the other by the Union. At one point, it's said, they fired on each other all night long, filling the inlet with cannonballs but falling short of hitting each other.

Fort Pickens is part of the Gulf Islands National Seashore, rich in wildlife and history and rimmed with the white cane-sugar beaches that the Panhandle is known for. It's worth a visit for the beaching, fishing, and nature watching for the 280 bird and animal species known to inhabit the area. Do take time to tour the fort's dingy dungeons and cool, brick corridors. Views of the Gulf and bay from the ramparts are unequaled, and the fort's past rings with battle lore and human drama, including the shameful story of the imprisonment here of warrior chief Geronimo.

Pensacola's history is rich and varied, but the chief reason to rush out here on the first available weekend is to see the National Museum of Naval Aviation, the largest naval aviation museum in the world. Indoors and out are eye-popping displays of aircraft of all sizes and types from the most rare—including a wooden leviathan that was the first aircraft to fly across the Atlantic—to classic carrier planes from every layer in naval aviation history. Make an entire day of this outstanding free attraction.

Plan your weekend with maps in hand because there is such a confusion of islands and place names. Santa Rosa Island, for example, which is fifty miles long and half a mile wide, holds a half dozen communities set in two counties. If it's a Gulf beach you want, be sure to make reservations at a Gulf-front property, not at a "waterfront" hotel, which could be on a sound, bay, or bayou. Trace out trips ahead of time to make sure you take the right bridge, or you could end up looking at your destination from across a narrow inlet.

The old L&N rail depot, built in downtown Pensacola in 1912, has been faithfully refurbished as a luxury hotel. The area also offers historic bed and breakfasts, chain motels, and long-term rentals in beachfront homes and condos.

Specifically: Contact the Chamber of Commerce, 1401 East Gregory Street, Pensacola, FL 32501, 800-874-1234 or 904-434-1234, for accommodations listings, maps, and brochures on attractions, dining, and events. On arrival, stop at the Welcome Center in Wayside Park at the north end of the Pensacola Bay Bridge for additional information.

25 Where Sun Meets Sea
Cedar Key

Nowhere in the Sunshine State are sunsets more glowingly golden than on Cedar Key, a low-lying island in the Gulf of Mexico miles from anywhere. The nearest city of any size is Gainesville, and that's an hour away. Detour off US 19/98, the highway that runs north and south along Florida's west coast, to drive the long causeway that seems to float atop a shimmering sea as it sails you to this enchanted island at the end of the road.

Driving the sleepy streets of Cedar Key today, you'll find it hard to imagine a time when this was a thriving seaport so important that the state's first railroad ran between here and the major seaport on the Atlantic side, Fernandina Beach. Named for the cedar trees that once covered the area, the key was denuded by foresters who sold the lumber to a company that made pencils.

During the Civil War, when salt was required as a preservative, the salt pans of Cedar Key were a war prize that went to the Union. Families, some of them still here, grew rich on the natural bounty from forest and sea. Today, homes built of oyster-shell tabby or the ornately turned woods of the Victorian era remember the glory days before highways and air lanes replaced sailing ships and stranded Cedar Key in a forgotten backwater.

Fisherfolk and spongers have never abandoned the lush fisheries of the area, and it wasn't long before naturalists, artists, and crafters took up the spaces that commercial interests had left empty. As early as 1867, John Muir wrote about his 1,000-mile walk to Cedar Key. Still today, the marshes and shallow seas are one of nature's grandest nurseries, hosting seabirds, shorebirds, ocean life, and estuarine species of all kinds.

73

Hire a boat to explore Cedar Keys National Wildlife Refuge, a group of limited-access islands off Cedar Key. On one of them is a lighthouse that was built in 1850 on the highest point in Florida. Others have long, white-sand beaches better than any on the mainland.

Between Yankeetown and Cedar Key, another limited-access area covers 31,000 acres of wetlands in the Waccasassa Bay State Preserve. Camp, canoe, and fish these waters in one of the state's most wildly beautiful settings. Another small state reserve, Cedar Key Scrub, has a few nature trails. Shell Mound Park has nature trails around a prehistoric Indian mound.

Take time for both the small museums. One is state operated and shows Indian artifacts and remains of the salt industry; the historical museum in town is the best place to hear about the island's few, but devastating, hurricanes. Fine galleries, boutiques, and some outstanding restaurants are also found downtown.

Specifically: Write the Chamber of Commerce, Box 610, Cedar Key, FL 32625, for a directory to restaurants, businesses, campgrounds, sightseeing, fishing guides, and lodgings. The Island Place, located on the colorful pier, offers one- and two-bedroom units by the night or week. Call 352-543-5306. Although most visitors drive in, there's a 2,300-foot hard-surface runway for private planes and marina slips for transient boaters. Cedar Key has no shopping centers, but basic supplies are available. If you're staying in a campground or self-catering apartment, bring at least some provisions with you.

26 Rough It on a Barrier Island
Cayo Costa

Cayo Costa Island in the Gulf of Mexico is not only one of the largest barrier islands in Florida; it's a state park where you can overnight in a cabin or in your own tent. A long finger of white-sand beaches and low green scrub, the island is the southern jaw of Boca Grande Pass, which has been famed for its tarpon fishing since the star drag reel was invented here generations ago.

Getting here is half the fun. You'll have to plan and bring all provisions and supplies, then get them here by boat. Or, if you don't care to overnight in the wilderness, take a day cruise that deposits you on the island in the morning and returns you to the mainland that afternoon. To get the real flavor of Cayo Costa, however, reserve one of the primitive cabins. After the day-trippers leave, you're alone on the island with the ranger, any fellow campers, the deserted beaches, a few wild pigs, and breathtaking sunrises and sunsets.

Work the low-tide line, especially after a storm, to find collages of colorful seashells: whelks, tellins, scallops in every shade from bright orange to variegated reds and soft beiges, tulip shells, auger shells, starfish, sand dollars, all displayed on a background of tumbled shell rubble that sometimes yields some of the rarest finds of all because the tiniest shells go unnoticed by collectors who pick up only the largest specimens. Yet, perfection in miniature, they are one of a shell fancier's greatest pleasures.

The list of bird sightings here reads like an Audubon who's who: roseate spoonbills, snowy egrets, great blue herons, loons, vultures, gulls, doves, cormorants, sandpipers, rare wood storks, and reddish egrets tiptoeing through the shallows in search of dinner while ospreys and pelicans soar overhead on fishing expeditions.

A snowy egret

Among the sabal palms, Australian pines, cabbage palm forests, and gumbo-limbo hammocks, you may see woodpeckers, jays, and owls; on the beach you may encounter a sea turtle laying her eggs. Loggerheads nest May to September. Keep your distance, and don't disturb either the turtles or any nest markers put out by park rangers.

Offshore, watch the surface for bottle-nosed dolphins. Pods of two, four, and more porpoises perform an almost nonstop show for sharp eyes, weaving and darting in search of small fry. Cayo Costa, far from the nearest highway, telephone, or TV cable, is one of those islands that many couples like to think of as their own.

Specifically: Lee County Visitor and Convention Bureau, 2180 West First Street, Fort Myers, FL 33902, 813-338-3500 or 800-533-4753. Cayo Costa Island State Preserve Park, Box 1150, Boca Grande, FL 33921, 813-964-0375.

27 Take a Collegiate Break
Gainesville

Although Gainesville often makes the top ten when magazines list the nation's best places to live or to retire, it has never made the tourism big leagues. That's what makes Alachua County an undiscovered hideaway for the couple seeking a break from the theme parks and beaches.

It's the home of the University of Florida, which swells the population by more than 34,000 when school is in session. It's unlikely that your travel agent will grab you by the lapels and give Gainesville the hard sell unless you want to come see a Gators game. Yet the city and the surrounding area have some of Florida's best and most unusual travel pleasures. Combine them with a football weekend, or plan your trip at another time, when Gainesville is just another small town.

For openers there are the county's twenty-three springs, all of them offering some added feature such as an historic building, campground, cave diving, geological oddities, or hiking paths. Most are open to the public for swimming in clear, sweet waters that stay the same temperature all year.

Hike the Devil's Millhopper, a geological wonderland in a 120-foot-deep sinkhole that shelters plants that grow nowhere else in Florida. Visit the Florida Museum of Natural History at the university to explore a full-size Florida limestone cave and a Mayan palace.

Paynes Prairie State Preserve is an 18,000-acre wildlife sanctuary with its own herd of bison. Its ponds and lakes twitter with thousands of migrating birds, including the sandhill crane, while alligators hunker in hidden lairs and wait their chance for a kill. An outdoorsy couple could spend an entire Gainesville weekend right here, hiking and birdwatching. Each April, a Walk Through Time at the prairie invites visitors to chat with Confederate soldiers, meet early Spanish settlers, and mingle with early Indian tribes.

Indian occupation of the prairie dates to 10,000 B.C. By the late seventeenth century the Spanish operated the largest cattle ranch in Florida on what naturalist William Bartram later called "the great Alachua Savannah." Most of the wildlife he described 200 years ago still thrives here.

When the Spanish came to the county in the early 1500s, they found it occupied by the Timucuans. Although St. Augustine was the chief Spanish stronghold, they had to reach far inland for farm products that were raised by agricultural tribes, and Spanish priests, equally eager to harvest souls, established missions for miles around.

Just southeast of Gainesville near Cross Creek find the rustic homestead where Marjorie Kinnan Rawlings, author of *The Yearling*, lived and wrote. A favorite afternoon outing for locals is to motor or bicycle country lanes in the area, then eat at The Yearling restaurant, whose recipes are selected from Rawlings's book *Cross Creek Cookery*. Specialties include cooter pie, gator tail, catfish, and local vegetables such as greens and yams.

From here, jog west to the village of Micanopy (mick-can-OH-pee), the oldest town in Florida. When the Spanish arrived, it was a Timucuan village; by the 1700s it was a Seminole settlement. In the 1800s it became a swank winter spa.

Today the old brick "downtown" is so faithful a scene that filmmakers came here to photograph live oaks towering among vivid Victorian homes and shops for such films as *Doc Hollywood* starring Michael J. Fox. In the Village Square Book Shop, Walter and Marie Winter have one of the state's best collections of Floridiana and antiquarian books.

Bring a picnic lunch to enjoy on the village green, or try

79

one of the local restaurants or snack bars. Then wander the shops to look for fine antiques, old sheet music, superb crafts, and Delectable Collectables where Monica Beth Fowler specializes in cameos and other antique jewelry.

Or drive north out of Gainesville to Waldo to see the vintage rail depot and more old brick mercantiles that are now filled with antiques. World War II buffs can continue a few miles farther north toward Starke with its curio shops and historic streets. During the war the town was a hangout for soldiers who were stationed at Camp Blanding, a story now told in the local historical museum.

Gainesville itself has a busy, college-town air with the usual hangouts: pubs, coffeehouses, bookstores, and restaurants that specialize in filling meals at modest prices. Hotels, too, are popular chains in the moderate price range, making your Gainesville weekend affordable as well as off the beaten path.

Specifically: Alachua County Visitors and Convention Bureau, 10 S.W. Second Avenue, Suite 220, Gainesville, FL 32601, 352-374-5260.

28 The World's Your Oyster
Apalachicola

Apalachicola oysters are featured on menus throughout Florida, so one reason to weekend in this quaint seaside village is to stuff yourself with some of the freshest, plumpest oysters in the state. The Gibson Inn, typical of turn-of-the-century wooden hotels, is still an unpretentious small-town hospitality center where memorable meals are served at modest prices. The three-story relic, built in 1907, has thirty-one rooms, private baths, and antique furnishings.

A protected river mouth on a chunk of mainland that noses out into the Gulf of Mexico, Apalachicola was a natural harbor that invited early settlement. As early as 18,000 years ago, primeval tribes thrived here on the sea's cornucopia. Scottish fur traders came to bargain with the Creeks; by 1822 the town was a major cotton port. Laid out on the plan of Philadelphia, the city burst at the seams in winter when cotton was shipped, then emptied almost to the last inhabitant during yellow fever season.

It was during one fever epidemic that John Gorrie, a local physician, invented an ice-making machine to cool his patients. A replica of his 1851 patent is on display at a small museum here. If you are history or architecture buffs, walk the neatly laid out streets past old homes, warehouses, churches, and shops dating to the early 1800s. It's fun to trace the city's various boom periods: cotton, then blockade running and salt, then lumber, and finally fishing, canning, and sponging. Except for some cotton warehouses that are in ruins, the waterfront looks much as it did a century ago.

For a pleasant afternoon on the windswept ramparts where the St. Marks and Wakulla rivers meet, take a picnic lunch to the San Marcos de Apalache State Historic Site.

Ramble through ruins that date to the earliest Spanish adventures here in the 1600s. A Spanish bombproof was built during 1750–1785; Andrew Jackson occupied the presidio here in 1818. Most buildings are from the Civil War era.

If natural history is more your cup of tea, come to the site anyway to stand on the observation deck overlooking the Wakulla. One of the richest nurseries in the state, the vast Apalachicola estuary, with its bayous and swamps, rivers and islands, teems with life.

Dozens of types of salamanders, frogs, turtles, lizards, snakes, waterfowl, songbirds, and migrating birds are spotted in the thousands of wetland acres in this area. Come to the reserves and preserves just to observe, photograph, or fish inshore or offshore. During hunting seasons, St. Vincent National Wildlife Refuge is open for the harvest of deer, wild pigs, and raccoons.

For some of the most spectacular beaches in the state, drive to St. George Island on the Gulf of Mexico or the St. Joseph Peninsula, which juts north from Cape San Blas. It was near here in 1942 that a British oil tanker was torpedoed by a German submarine. Volunteers rushed out in their own boats from Apalachicola to pick up survivors, rescuing fourteen of the forty-seven who had been aboard. The hulk of *Sea Dream*, one of the boats used in the rescue, is on display at the waterfront in town.

The old downtown area is trying hard to attract antiquers and shoppers. Except during local festivals, though, it is uncrowded and natural–an ideal place for unhurried shopping, jawboning with friendly locals, and soaking up the southern, small-town flavor.

Souvenir shops in the area sell a T-shirt printed with a map of Apalachicola and the surrounding terrain from St. Marks to Tate's Hell. It is titled "Florida's Forgotten Coast."

Once discovered by the weekend traveler, however, it is never forgotten again.

Specifically: Write the Chamber of Commerce, 57 Market Street, Apalachicola, FL 32329, 904-653-9419, for lists of campgrounds and hotels. Request maps and brochures on history, nature, fishing and hunting, sailing, and any other special interests.

29 Beyond the Gator Bowl
Jacksonville

It's called America's First Coast because America's first settlers came ashore here, but the Jacksonville area is also a first
Florida stop for visitors arriving from the north on I-95. Most
keep right on trucking, not realizing that Jacksonville and its
beaches are Florida's most under-appreciated, untouristy,
dynamite destination.

If you're a football fan, you already know about the
annual Florida-Georgia game, which has been a sellout at the
82,000-seat Gator Bowl since 1933. It's played each year in
late October or early November. The Outback Steakhouse
Gator Bowl Classic, hosting top college teams, is the city's
other football blockbuster, played during the New Year holidays. Book well in advance for these weekends; the city
bulges at the seams.

Except for the beaches, which are best in summer, there is
no "season" as there is in south Florida. This is probably
Florida's most homogeneous city, an even mix of industry,
entertainment, attractions, shopping, old and new neighborhoods, historic sites, and a nice mix of young and old, singles
and couples.

From your weekend "home" base in one of the bed and
breakfasts, such as the St. Johns House in the Avondale

Historic District or the Archibald in the Springfield Historic District, set out to explore some of the state's oldest historic sites and best museums. Then spend the evenings downtown on the river, where water taxis are your designated driver among restaurants, clubs, and boutiques on both sides of the St. Johns.

Or take in a performance at the Alhambra Dinner Theater, which stages Broadway musicals. Check the newspaper for the city's many cultural attractions. Jacksonville has its own symphony, ballet, opera companies, and professional theaters.

Among the city's world-class museums is one of the nation's five Karpeles Manuscript Library museums. At the Cummer Gallery of Art, see more than 2,000 works in twelve galleries, then see the Jacksonville Art Museum with its Picassos and pre-Columbian art, the fire museum, a martime museum, a museum of science and history, and a museum of southern history. Jacksonville also has one of the South's best zoos. A few miles south lies Marineland, the state's first marine attraction. See the performing dolphins, a 3-D film, and an important seashell collection.

If you want to get out on the water, charter a sportfishing boat, or fish from the 983-foot pier on Jacksonville Beach. The Mayport Ferry, which is a shortcut route across the St. Johns River between Jacksonville and Mayport, is one of the best cruise bargains in the state. Take your car for $2.50, bicycles for 50 cents.

Book La Cruise for a day on the Atlantic with casino gambling, dining first at La Cruise Restaurant, which for years was a Mayport landmark known as Strickland's. At the Mayport Naval Air station, home of the USS *Saratoga*, free tours of ships, including aircraft carriers, are offered on weekend afternoons.

To get the flavor of the area's earliest years, visit Fort

Caroline, which dates to the region's first settlers. French Huguenots, they were slaughtered by invading Spaniards. At Kingsley Plantation, see the plantation manor and slave quarters of what was once a giant empire covering thousands of acres. It's now part of the Timucuan Ecological and Historic Preserve, with ranger programs provided by the National Park Service.

Specifically: Convention and Visitors Bureau, 3 Independent Drive, Jacksonville, FL 32202, 904-798-9148. Request brochures on accommodations, dining, sightseeing, beaches, museums, history, tours, shopping, fishing, and other interests.

30 Make Friends with a Manatee

You might be gliding silently in a canoe, sitting on a dock low to the river, or keeping watch on a boardwalk over a spring. Suddenly a manatee sounds, so close that you can smell its moist breath and count its wirelike whiskers. Once introduced to manatee watching, you are hooked. Discover the manatee world together and begin a lifelong love affair – at least with the manatee.

Prepare to be disillusioned. Manatees stink, they're incredibly ugly, and it's darned annoying when they honk wet stuff all over you. Yet you just can't help but love these homely, shy, sluggish, curious cows of the sea.

They breathe air and drink mother's milk just as we do. Their closest relatives are the elephant and the African hyrax; their brothers are called dugong in Australia. Another relative, the Stellar's sea cow, was found in the Bering Sea in the 1700s and hunted to extinction. Now Florida's manatees, too, are being hounded, hurt, and displaced to the point where they, too, may disappear within the next generation.

Because manatees, like porpoises, surface to breathe air and have a look at the sky, humans can't help feeling a kinship with them. Unlike porpoises, they are much harder to find in the wild. Unexpected sightings are rare and exciting, but you can increase your chances of seeing one by seeking out their favorite haunts. Kings Bay near Crystal River, where thirty springs pour into a massive bay, is one of the most popular scuba sites in the Sunshine State. Here, waters that stay 72 degrees year-round create a cozy playground where manatees and divers can get a good look at each other. Divers or boats aren't permitted in manatees refuge areas at Blue Springs near Orange City in central Florida, but the state park

Homely, lovable manatees

has boardwalks and overlooks that offer a clear view of manatee swimming below.

Rental boats and canoes are available at many spots along the St. Johns River. The best sightings are upriver between Sanford and DeLand. Idle for hours along the weedy edges of rivers and spring runs, hoping that a manatee will bumble along in search of a mouthful of water hyacinth and belch some your way.

For a sure sighting, look up a manatee in captivity. Injured manatees are brought to the Homosassa Springs State Wildlife Park, about sixty miles north of Tampa, for rehabilitation. View them in an underwater observatory. A manatee rehab center has also been added to the Lowry Park Zoo in Tampa.

Sea World's "Manatees: The Last Generation?" is a massive, emotionally moving exhibit at Sea World in Orlando. See the film. Then watch as manatees maneuver around their own lagoon, suckle their young, and goggle at the world above the surface each time they come up for a gulp of air.

Manatees grow as long as 15 feet, weigh an elephantine 1,000 pounds or more, and can live in captivity for 30 years or so. All they want out of life is a lazy river, fresh water to drink, and a hundred pounds of vegetation to chomp through each day. Yet their numbers are dwindling as they tangle with traps and collide with boat props. It's thought that only a scant 2,000 or fewer remain.

If you're looking for a low-key, next-to-nature Florida jaunt, go looking for manatees. Even if you don't find one, you'll discover a placid river or a crystal spring where manatees might be found, next time.

Specifically: Write the Florida Department of Natural Resources, Douglas Building #642, Tallahassee, FL 32399 and request a list of sites where manatees are most likely to be sighted. Ask, too, for brochures listing your other interests that will mesh with a manatee watch such as camping, boating, scuba diving, or fishing. Rules vary regarding manatee observation, diving, and boats according to the place and the time of year. Respect them. Admission is charged to Sea World, Lowry Park Zoo, and other sites where manatees are displayed.

31 Plush Pleasures of the Palm Beaches

Ever since the turn of the century, when rail magnate Henry Flagler strung a series of spendthrift hotels down the east coast of the Sunshine State, Palm Beach has been synonymous with conspicuous consumption. His landmark, The Breakers, with its Italian Renaissance opulence, has for decades been a favorite with the elite of New York, Hollywood, and even London. In nearby Boca Raton, the Boca Raton Hotel and Club was built by rival developer Addison Mizner to challenge The Breakers; the two remain among the most posh resorts in the state.

Equally splendid and newer on the beachfront scene is the small (212-room) Ocean Grand, which has become as well known for its cuisine as for its suave, European-style service. There's also a Ritz-Carlton on the beach as well as a handful of intimate, very tony hotels a block or two inland from the beach.

Well inland, but no less high-toned, is the Palm Beach Polo and Country Club with a guest list that reads like a Who's Who of International Polo. Visitors are welcome to drop in and watch the chuckers, but call ahead for times and dates.

Three basic budget decisions determine the time that's right for you to tackle Palm Beach. To see and be seen, arrive in December when The Season bursts on the scene. The island's wealthy (names have included the Kennedys, Trumps, and Posts) come south and air out their mansions. Glittering balls and other fund-raisers bring in millions of dollars. Shops along Worth Avenue display their most exclusive, expensive togs and baubles.

The Montreal Expos and Atlanta Braves are in spring training at the West Palm Beach Municipal Stadium. Opera,

Broadway musicals, and ballet play the magnificent Kravits Center for the Performing Arts. It's the most exciting, relevant time to be here, with princely prices to match.

May and October, shoulder seasons, bring some of the area's best beach weather. Hotel tariffs take a dip and reservations in the better restaurants are easier to get, but the Beautiful People are starting to drift back to the Hamptons, Newport, and Martha's Vineyard. Creative packages make your dollars stretch now, with such extras included as greens fees, a gourmet dinner or two, or unlimited court time.

In summer your fellow guests are apt to be more ordinary folks. You'll see more conference attendees and other group travelers at your hotel. Some of the tonier restaurants and shops may be closed, and days are too hot for more than a desultory game of tennis or golf.

However, there are compensations. Traffic and crowds are lighter, resort rates are at rock bottom (which can still mean $200 a night or more for a double at the best hotels), sizzling concerts and other special events are scheduled to entice travelers to come in summer, and Clearance Sale signs go up at the best shops. A younger crowd comes to play, so you'll feel the tempo pick up as honeymooners and chic young families make the scene.

Best of all are the water sports on a calm, cool ocean that in winter can turn cold and rough. Scuba diving on Judo Ledge, Kreuger's Reef, Loggerhead Run, Horseshoe Reef, and half a dozen wrecks is superb. It seems fitting in Palm Beach that one of the artificial reefs is a Rolls-Royce Silver Shadow that was deep-sixed in 1985 and is now a refuge for clouds of colorful fish.

Whatever time of year you weekend in Palm Beach, reserve some time for sightseeing. Whitehall, the palatial mansion built by rail magnate Henry Flagler, rivals the stately homes of England. Rent a bicycle at your hotel to explore the ocean drives and shaded streets, where you might spot a celebrity or two. Behind the hedges and fences, their mansions can't be seen from the road, but you may run into one at a shop or a favorite hangout. Take a sightseeing cruise; mansions that can't be seen from the road can be seen from the water.

Book a luxury cruise out of the Port of Palm Beach. It's one of the state's most uncrowded cruise ports, which means easier parking and faster embarkation/debarkation. And don't miss Boca Raton's International Museum of Cartoon Art, which is the largest and most important collection of cartoon art and animation in the world.

Specifically: Request the Palm Beach County Visitors Guide from the Convention and Visitors Bureau, 1555 Palm Beach Lakes Boulevard, Suite 204, West Palm Beach, FL 33401, 407-471-3995.

32 Lost in Space

Except for its one, stupendous tourist attraction–NASA Kennedy Space Center Spaceport USA–the Cape Canaveral area remains one of Florida's most undiscovered vacation playlands. People pop in on a side trip from Orlando's theme parks or to overnight on their way to south Florida, never quite discovering this area's seventy-two miles of ravishing beaches and its richness of wildlife.

Visiting the Spaceport is a definite must, but it's adequately covered by other guidebooks. What else might you do on a Space Coast weekend? Start with offbeat lodgings at the Great Outdoors in Titusville. It's a complete RV community with its own golf, tennis, pool, fishing, boating, planned activities, and shops. If you don't have an RV, rent one of the permanently installed, park-model RVs. It's like having a spacious, fully furnished apartment for the price of a hotel room, with the advantage of the instant camaraderie shared by the camping brotherhood.

If you'd rather stay on the beach, Cocoa Beach is lined with oceanfront showplaces, including a Hilton, Days Inn, Howard Johnson, and Holiday Inn.

Reserve an afternoon for grazing your way around Historic Cocoa Village, downtown Cocoa. Merchants moved to outlying malls, leaving the old part of town to be revitalized by imaginative young entrepreneurs. Streets now are lined with galleries, unique shops, sidewalk cafés, and smart restaurants. During its festivals, it sings. Other days, there's a pleasant hum.

A piano player plays jazz on the sidewalk. Lovers stroll past shop windows, then stop for lunch in a hidden courtyard. An elderly couple rests on a park bench, the sun

Blast off at the Cape

backlighting silver hair. Passers-by stop to read posters at a stately old movie palace, now the home of a local playhouse. The village was settled in the 1860s; the restoration re-creates the look and feel of the 1920s.

By far the most glittering gem in the cape's diadem is its nature show, and it's free. Playalinda Beach, secluded and sea-swept, is a part of the sprawling Canaveral National Seashore. Park the car in a free lot; then take boardwalks across the fragile dunes to find miles of beach and picnic area along the Atlantic.

Merritt Island National Wildlife Refuge has one of the most varied bird populations in the nation, including more threatened and endangered species than can be found at any other wildlife refuge in the United States. Stop at the visitors center to view exhibits and pick up brochures; then take your binoculars on the self-guided walking trails and driving routes.

Sebastian Inlet State Recreation Area, with its crashing coamers, is one of the best surfing areas in the state. It's surrounded by a 576-acre state park with camping, swimming, boating, diving, and picnicking. Indian River Lagoon is the most diverse estuarine environment in the nation. Come here to view more than 300 endangered species, including almost 2,800 species of animals, 685 species of fish, 310 kinds of birds, and 1,350 different plants. This is also a great park for surfing, sailing, sunning, and picnicking.

Even if you're not an angler, come to the historic Cocoa Beach Pier for the salty seafood restaurants, music and entertainments, and a nonstop festival air. Or go airboating through a cypress swamp west of the cape. You float freely as if flying, just millimeters above the surface, as you speed through grasses and shallows that teem with wildlife.

Come for the space shots, IMAX movie, Astronaut Hall of Fame, and all the rest, but don't miss an equally exciting chance to spend a weekend under nature's wing.

Specifically: Space Coast Office of Tourism, 2725 St. Johns Street, Viera, FL 32940, 800-USA-1969 or 407-633-2110. Ask for maps, brochures, and lists of lodgings throughout the area, which includes Titusville, Cocoa Beach, Melbourne, and Palm Bay. For information on the Great Outdoors, call 407-269-5004.

33 From Cigars to Soho
Ybor City

It began at the turn of the century as a community of immigrants, exiles, and cigar factories where Jose Marti roused the workers with fiery speeches demanding the liberation of Cuba. When the Spanish-American War erupted, it was here that Teddy Roosevelt recruited and trained his famous Rough Riders for the triumphant charge up San Juan Hill.

Today the Ybor City section of Tampa is the Soho of the South, one of the trendiest nightspots in the state and a daytime beehive of shopping and historic tours. Come for a weekend of pleasant culture shock.

Don Vincente Martinez Ybor opened his first cigar factory here in 1886, and cigar makers poured in from all over the world. Soon 12,000 people were hand-rolling 500 million stogies a year.

Florida's oldest restaurant, the Columbia, opened here in 1905. Today it's a chain, but the original in Ybor (say EE-bore) City remains one of Tampa's most beloved culinary and architectural landmarks. It's still in the Hernandez family, now on its fourth generation as restaurateurs. Go whole hog by ordering the Columbia salad, black bean soup, paella, and flan for a Cuban feast without equal.

A newspaper, *La Gaceta*, began publishing in 1922 in English, Spanish, and Italian. Still published weekly, it's the only trilingual newspaper in the United States. Drop in at La Tropicana Cafe, its unofficial office, to get the latest buzz and a cup of Cuban coffee.

Machines took over the making of cigars and, except for a small cult following, cigars themselves went the way of the silent movie and the vaudeville comedian. More than 200 cigar factories, filling 110 blocks in the middle of Tampa, lay on history's trash heap until a hip new generation discovered it and turned it into 110 blocks of too much fun. That's where you and your weekend come in.

Spend days in funky shops, bookstores, boutiques, and galleries. Linger in sidewalk cafés sipping espresso. Lunch on Cuban sandwiches made with Cuban bread that is still baked at La Segunda Central with the traditional palm leaf on each loaf. Dine around in smart restaurants, ending your evening at a piano bar or a flamenco performance. Nightly dance shows are given at the Columbia Monday through Saturday.

Miami has its own ethnic energy with elements from all over Central and South America and the Caribbean. Key West has its arty wackiness, with Cuban overtones. St. Augustine has the flavor of old Spain. Ybor City, by contrast, is a unique blend of old Cuba, old Italy, and old Tampa with a rollerblade pace and a trendy, up-market garnish.

The El Pasaje Plaza/Cherokee Club, once an elite "gentlemen's club," now houses a Creole restaurant serving New Orleans food and jazz. Eat indoors surrounded by wood wainscoting and sculptured ceilings, or outdoors in the flower-scented brick courtyard. Sunday brunch is an Event.

The Corner Cafe, where cigar workers gathered for coffee and gossip, is the site of the original Columbia, which now covers an entire block. In Latin Plaza, families still come once a year to cover a statue with flowers in honor of their mothers. Dominoes are still played in the Italian Club by distinguished descendants of some of Tampa's first settlers. The Ballet Folklorico de Ybor teaches flamenco and other traditional dances of Spain, Italy, Cuba, Mexico, and the Caribbean. San Do Designs does Spanish tiles.

On the corner of 13th Street and 7th Avenue, La Union Marti-Maceo is the club formed long ago for Afro-Cubans. It was one of the many mutual aid societies that were an important part of the social structure in immigrant societies.

Las Novedades, built in 1917 and once a famous restaurant, is now the home of the sizzling Tracks nightclub. Another nightclub now fills the historic Ritz Theater, an ornate movie palace built in 1917.

The original V.M. Ybor Cigar Company is now Ybor Square, a collection of craft shops and restaurants. The old post office is now the site of the Blue Ribbon Grocery. The Bank of Ybor City today houses modern art.

To get a true insider's look at Ybor City, start with a guided walking tour through a thriving Latin enclave of homes, factories, churches, banks, clubs, and shops. Then strike out on your own, taking time to slip into dusty shops and to talk to talented artisans. Laze in the shade of an old church to watch old men play dominoes.

Visit the Ybor City State Museum on 9th Avenue and tour Preservation Park to see the restored "shotgun" homes. Typical of the thousands of simple three-room cottages that housed thousands of immigrants, they gained their name because a shotgun could be fired through the front door and out the back door without hitting anything. Each had a sitting room in front, a bedroom in the middle, and a kitchen in the rear. On every front porch was a long, sharp nail on which a deliveryman hung a fresh loaf of Cuban bread each morning.

Ybor City is a favorite spot for special events, street dances, concerts, and ethnic festivals, all of them worth a weekend. Still, it's the ordinary nights in this extraordinary place that you'll remember best.

Specifically: Call 800-44-TAMPA for information and maps or write the Convention and Visitors Bureau, 111 Madison Street, Suite 1010, Tampa, FL 33602. Ybor City is bounded by 15th and 21st Streets and 7th and Palm Avenues. To book a walking tour, call 813-223-1111, ext. 46. Handy hotels include the Tampa Regency Westshore, known for its thirty-five-acre bird sanctuary and two of the city's best restaurants (reservations 800-233-1234), and the Wyndham Harbour Island Hotel in the heart of the chic Harbour Island Shops (reservations 800-822-4200).

34 Exploring by Houseboat
St. Johns River

Florida is the year-round yachting capital of the Americas, where port cities host huge fleets of sportfishing boats and blue-water sailboats. Rent one and play captain and crew, but only if you're experienced sailors with the credentials to satisfy both the rental firm and its insurance company.

If you're not certified sailors, rent a houseboat. No boating experience is required. You'll have the privacy and freedom of a bareboat, the comforts of a fully equipped floating home, and a price tag that is less than you'd pay at a top resort for accommodations, meals, and water sports. Rental houseboats are available in several Florida waterways, including the Everglades, the Kissimmee River out of River Ranch, the Keys, and other locales.

One of the best, offering sheltered waters and a nature show par excellence, is the St. Johns River. The river itself is navigable by commercial barges from its mouth at Mayport/Jacksonville to Sanford, which lies 150 miles upstream. Houseboat rentals, however, are centered well upriver in the DeLand area, and the boats are usually not permitted to go farther north than Palatka.

This gives you more water than you can explore in a weekend because there's the river itself plus side routes into marinas, lakes, streams, and springs. Take a side trip into Dunn's Creek or stop at Welaka to see the State Fish Preserve. Fish for stripers at Croaker Hole Cove.

Go ashore at Palatka to hike ravishing Ravine Gardens. In the spring the slopes and gorges are covered with azaleas in bloom. Walk the charming downtown area to shop for provisions, and tour the historic Bronson-Mulholland House. At Blue Spring State Park, a favorite winter home of manatees, hike a boardwalk deep into the scrub, then swim in the spring's crystal waters. Tour the home of the original settlers and picnic under a live oak tree.

Wave as the Rivership *Romance*, a gingerbread excursion paddlewheeler, whirs past. Nose into end-of-the-world fish camps. Stop at waterfront restaurants, where plastic basins filled with sweet and steamy blue crabs are served on newspaper-covered tables. Look for the rotted stubs of old pilings, indicating where piers once reached into the river to welcome steamboats. Look high into the trees where you'll see distinctly round, dark green clumps. Then steal a kiss, because they are wild mistletoe.

Just north of Lake George, look for the antebellum home overlooking the river at Marker 65. It was built by a Union officer, an outpost for stopping Confederate blockade runners. At idle speed, steal along the banks to watch the woods for raccoons, cormorants, anhingas, wild monkeys, and raptors. Along the shoreline are endless chances to photograph egrets, herons, ibis, sleepy alligators, and armies of turtles sunning on half-submerged logs.

At Deadman's Bend, look for a sign indicating that you're in the Lake Woodruff Bird Sanctuary. You may want to come back later from the land side and continue your bird-watching from hiking paths. Maintain a constant lookout for manatees, which could be spotted anywhere in the river.

Stop at Hontoon Island, where you can overnight at the marina if you like, to climb the ninety-foot observation tower for a bird's-eye view of the snaking St. Johns stretching from horizon to horizon. A replica of a rare owl totem, carved by Timucuan Indians in about A.D. 1300 and uncovered here, can be seen in the 1,650-acre island park. Now in a museum, the original is said to be the only true totem ever uncovered east of the Pacific coastal range.

One word of advice. Houseboats are usually designed to sleep a crowd, dorm-style, sharing one bathroom. If you're looking for a romantic weekend afloat, don't be tempted to split the costs with other couples. You'll want this floating island all to yourselves.

Specifically: Houseboat rentals on the St. Johns are available from Hontoon Landing Resort and Marina, 2317 River Road, DeLand, FL 32720, 904-734-2474 or 800-248-2474. Three-night midweek rentals are the best buy. Weekend rentals run from Friday afternoon to Sunday afternoon. Mini-weekend rentals run from Saturday 10:00 A.M. to Sunday at 4:00 P.M.

35 Dogfight in the Skies
Kissimmee

Shoot him down in flames. Blast her out of the skies. Work off your aggressions, test your flight prowess, and have the most wildly exciting weekend of your lives! The two of you really *can* dogfight in real airplanes on a real flight, even if you don't know the first thing about piloting. Here's how it works.

The airplanes flown by Fighter Pilots USA are swift, agile SAIA Marchettis used as fighter trainers by NATO and in search and rescue by many nations of the world. They're tough—able to pull more Gs than most humans can stand—and they fly at lightning speeds in the 270 mph range.

According to the pilots, all of them highly trained fighter jocks, you can't get the airplane into anything that they can't get you out of. Top gun is Tim DesMarais, Lt. Col. USAF (Ret). His fighter pilots include Woodstock, Strudel, Mo, Stealth, and Iceman, all of them retired or reserve U.S. Air Force officers who still have the right stuff.

The sky is the limit. They've flown passengers as young as age nine and as old as ninety-two. The only limit may be size: 275 pounds is about as much passenger as they like to load. Shove the stick any way you choose; when you can't take any more, call "Knock it off" and your pilot will tidy up the attitude until you're comfortable again.

The duel begins in a ground school briefing much like that given to fighter pilots. You're introduced to the lingo, with vivid instructions about keeping tally-ho and neutralizing the bandit. Lose sight of the bandit and it's no-joy. If you can't kill, survive. Don't be a smoking hole. Speed is life. Lose sight, lose fight. No guts, no glory. There are no points for second place.

You learn the rules of engagement. A hard deck of 2,000 feet MSL and VFR weather conditions must be maintained.

A 500-foot bubble must be maintained around each aircraft. Front-quarter gun attacks ahead of the wingline are not permitted. Head-on passes should clear to the right, nose high. It sounds daunting, but by the time you're ready to strap on the seat belt, it all makes sense and you're ready for the kill.

The flight and fight are real. The only difference is that, while real fighters have only enough ammo to last about six seconds, you're limited only by fuel ("pushing dead dinosaurs out the back") and by the film that will record your derring-do and determine if either of you made a kill.

The contest ends with a debriefing that is even more fun than the briefing. "Lie, lie, lie, deny, deny, deny," advises your instructor in the briefing. "Cheat, sell your mother, but never admit they got on your tail." If the camera didn't catch it, you're home free. In the end, you get custody of the tape and both of you get Air Combat Certificates.

It's the best and most unusual weekend you've ever had with your clothes on.

Specifically: Call 407-931-4333. Fighter Pilots USA is at Kissimmee Municipal Airport, 3033 West Patrick Street, Kissimmee, FL 34741. Several programs are offered, starting at about $750 per person. Thousands of hotel and motel rooms are found nearby (Kissimmee is the gateway to Walt Disney World). For Kissimmee reservations, call 800-333-KISS. For more information, contact the Kissimmee–Saint Cloud Convention and Visitors Bureau, Box 422007, Kissimmee, FL 34742, 800-831-1844 or 407-847-5000.

36 Weekend to Weekend
The Love Boat

When you're lucky enough to have two weekends back to back, seize the opportunity for the romantic liaison of a lifetime aboard a "love boat" on a Caribbean cruise. Cruising is a natural for couples who travel together. However, it's also the most exciting way to date if you're not yet ready to share quarters. Each of you can have your own cabin, arranging to meet for meals, shore excursions, activities, parties, dancing, and watching sunrises and sunsets on deck. One cabin or two, you're together on a "love boat" and wonderful things will happen.

Florida is the cruising capital of the nation. Miami, Fort Lauderdale, Canaveral, and Tampa throb with the comings and goings of ocean liners on their way to and from the Panama Canal, the Caribbean, and all sorts of wanderings around the world. You can sail from Florida any day of the week to almost anywhere in the seven seas.

Some ships sail out of Florida only in winter, then go to Alaska for the summer. Some touch Florida ports only once a year or so on itineraries that continue to the South Pacific, the Aegean, the Mediterranean, or to South America and the Antarctic. In any case, there are many love boats but just one Love Boat company of television fame. It's Princess Cruise Lines.

Actually an enormous fleet that includes the *Crown Princess*, *Fair Princess*, *Golden Princess*, *Regal Princess*, the new *Sun Princess*, and many others, Princess is much more than the ship featured in the TV series. Seasoned cruisers have their favorite ships and will follow them anywhere. Let's focus for now, however, on a route.

Princess ships sail two popular itineraries out of Fort Lauderdale. Seven-day cruises of the eastern Caribbean call at such ports as St. Maarten with its Dutch heritage, St. Thomas in the U.S. Virgin Islands, and the Princess Cays in the Bahamas. When the ships sail to the western Caribbean, they call at the Princess Cays, Montego Bay in Jamaica, the British crown colony of Grand Cayman, and the exotic island of Cozumel off Mexico's Yucatan peninsula.

Today's cruise liners are larger than many resorts, and they offer far more: round-the-clock activities, lounges with dancing and live entertainment, banquets and buffets, two and three swimming pools and several spas, fitness centers and gyms, two lavish stage shows a night, room service, movie theaters, a casino, duty-free shops, a library, remote-control TV in each cabin, and a cabin attendant who tidies up your room and brings fresh ice and fruit at least twice a day — all included in the price! The only extras are tips, bar drinks, and shore excursions.

Luxury liners have been built to be floating palaces since the days when ocean crossings took days. Atrium lobbies are three or more stories high, and they glow with marble and brass. Princess public rooms are decorated with fortunes in antiques and paintings. Furnishings are plush; meals are served on china and crystal by polished waiters. Decks are rich teak and, on spacious sports decks, you can play volleyball, basketball, or paddle tennis. One deck usually doubles as a jogging track.

Every cruise line has its own personality. The magic formula in a Princess cruise begins with the utter opulence of your surroundings and the excitement of one or two formal nights per week. Add cozy touches such as turndown service with a mint on your pillow, fresh towels twice a day, and starchy napkins in the posh dining room. Service is caring and correct; staff are a United Nations of bright and capable young men and women who speak many languages. Officers are seasoned seamen, trained at the world's top maritime academies. The pampering is total, from the moment you fall under the Princess spell until you're back on terra firma again.

Princess, like many of the better cruise lines, does not offer cruises shorter than one week. But this one is worth waiting for. After all, this isn't a cruise. It's the Love Boat.

Specifically: Consult a travel agent who is a member of ASTA (American Society of Travel Agents). Airfare and transfer from the airport to the ship and back are often included in the price.

37 Monkey Around in Miami

It all began with another couple who loved monkeys. In 1933, Connecticut residents Grace and Joseph DuMond – he was an animal behaviorist – released six Java monkeys into the steamy wilderness of a dense hammock in south Dade County. When funds for his research became scarce during the depression, DuMond began charging 10 cents admission to visitors who wanted to see the wild macaques.

Territorial in nature, the Javas resented this intrusion and began to defend their turf. So DuMond, unwilling to cage his animals, caged the people instead. Today, visitors roam the jungle in screened walkways; the monkeys still roam free, providing research for conservationists and endless merriment for onlookers.

Nature has taken its course. Today the original six have grown to a family of more than eighty Javas. They live here with more than 300 other primates in one of the few protected habitats for endangered primates in the United States. It is, say the owners, the only one where the public is welcome to join the fun.

Come in the morning and plan to stay all day because this place is unpredictable, endlessly entertaining, even addictive. Many area residents buy season passes; others sign on in the volunteer program.

A high point of the day is feeding time at a pool where Java monkeys, who are skilled fishermen, dive into the water to gather up their dinner. Unlike polished animal acts featuring trained critters, the Ape Encounter here is impromptu. Chimps and orangutans do their own thing while delighted audiences look on. Also to be seen in the Jungle, which is still owned by the DuMond family, are gibbons, guenons, spider monkeys, and the golden lion tamarin, which is threatened

*At the monkey jungle, you're in the cage
and the monkeys are loose*

with extinction. One tamarin that was born here has already been released into the wild. In all, about thirty-five species are housed and protected here.

In the four-acre Amazonian Rainforest, Upper Amazonian monkeys live in a forest of native South American plants, which will take years to recover completely from its destruction by the hurricane in 1992. This living laboratory has been an important breeding haven for South American primates. Many births here have been first-in-captivity births for rare and endangered species. The DuMonds' research in squirrel monkey reproduction is considered to be one of the classic works in primatology.

By happy coincidence, it was discovered during clean-up operations after Hurricane Andrew that the Jungle site is also an archaeological treasure trove. Eons ago as sinkholes developed, animals were caught in natural limestone traps. Digs here have uncovered bone and shell tools. Burned bones show primitive peoples cooked game on the site, and thousands of bones have been found from such extinct animals as the short-faced cave bear, Pleistocene horse, saber-toothed tiger, camel, bison, and dire wolf. With 5,000 specimens already found, it's proving to be the richest fossil deposit in south Florida.

As long as this is an atypical weekend for a rushing, cosmopolitan city like Miami, you may as well stay in an unusual inn too. Historic inns are common in most of Florida; in the concrete canyons of Miami they are a rarity. The Miami River Inn in East Little Havana was built in 1906 on the Miami River right across from the center of downtown. Northerners arrived on Flagler's railroad, hired horse and wagon to take themselves and their steamer trunks across the bridge to the inn, and stayed the winter. Beachfront hotels were still a distant dream.

A fenced, verdant oasis with its own pool, whirlpool, and tropic garden, the hotel was restored in the 1980s by local preservationist Sallye Jude, now the innkeeper. It's the oldest continuously operating inn south of St. Augustine.

Now a historic showplace, the inn has forty antique-furnished rooms and a few cottages and apartments. Breakfast is served in the cozy breakfast cottage or in the garden. When you arrive, you're offered a glass of wine to enjoy in the lobby library of historic publications and Miami information.

For nightlife, you're only a few blocks away from downtown, the Calle Ocho (Eighth Street) Latin area, shops, and galleries. Metrorail is just across the bridge; Bayside Festival Marketplace is only a stop or two away.

Write ahead for maps and instructions. Both these sites are well off the beaten path.

Specifically: Miami River Inn, 118 S.W. South River Drive, Miami, FL 33130, 305-325-0045. Monkey Jungle, 14805 S.W. 216th Street, Miami, FL 33170, 305-235-1611.

Winter

38 Next to Nature in Naples

Named for another seaside gem on the Mediterranean, Naples in Florida's southwestern corner has all the compelling charm of a Gulf-side village plus the advantage of lying at the end of the road in remote, sunlit splendor. It's an ideal weekend destination from the Miami or Fort Myers area but its distance from most other Florida cities keeps it aloof and exclusive.

Nature knocks at Naples's back door, and beaches lap at its front door. To the west is endless horizon, with magnificent Gulf sunsets nightly. To the south are the Ten Thousand Islands. Whatever your idea of a Florida weekend getaway indoors or out, luxury or spendthrift, Naples beckons.

If you're an ecotourist, visit the vast wildernesses of Big Cypress Swamp and the Everglades. Hike, boat, camp, and airboat through countless lakes, miles of sawgrass, boardwalk trails, and mazes of waterways to fill a nature notebook with sightings: bald eagles, bobcats, 200-year-old bald cypress trees, alligators, sandhill cranes, manatees, peregrine falcons, and twenty-four kinds of wild orchids.

The National Audubon Society's Corkscrew Swamp Sanctuary, twenty miles north of Naples, is an 11,000-acre nature preserve best known as a winter nesting area for wood storks.

117

In Collier-Seminole State Park, hike a nature trail through a salt marsh and highlands filled with tropical hardwoods, or canoe a 13.5-mile river trail.

In town, the Conservancy Nature Center offers guided trail tours, self-guided tours, and free nature cruises on the Gordon River. Staffed by volunteers, the conservancy works miracles in rehabilitating sick and injured wildlife and puts on a whale of a free exhibit with many hands-on displays. It's a must for wildlife lovers who are at first disappointed, then pleased to realize that these wild creatures have no names and are not turned into pets. They get minimal human association and, as soon as they're well enough, are put back into nature's family where they belong.

Rookery Bay National Estuarine Research Reserve south of town is 9,400 acres of mangrove swamp, pine flatwoods, and salt marshes straddled by boardwalks. See it all on foot or on a guided canoe tour. Or if you'd rather go sportfishing offshore aboard a sleek yacht, Naples has one of the state's most select fleets of professionally captained charter boats.

If your idea of the outdoors tends more to barefoot walks on the beach and nights in a luxurious hotel, Naples is the home of the splendid five-star, five-diamond Ritz-Carlton, where suites on the luxury level are in the $1,000 range, and the smart, four-star Registry resort, where you can take each other's photos in front of the impressive fountain in the atrium lobby and order a box lunch to take to the beach.

Even if this isn't your honeymoon, ask about honeymoon packages. Both resorts sprawl across spacious, manicured grounds filled with tropical flowers and rustling palms; both offer intensive tennis programs as well as golf privileges, swimming pools, water sports, fitness centers, and a choice of superb restaurants and lounges. For budget travelers the city has a selection of chain motels, including a Quality Inn with its own eighteen-hole golf club.

A favorite of wealthy Midwesterners who have built winter homes here, Naples has always had a silver spoon in its mouth. Shop for smart resort wear and accessories, choose among a dozen three-star restaurants, and jog on seven miles of uncrowded beach. If you'd rather get down and dirty, come in late May or late October to cheer the Swamp Buggy Championship Races. Specially designed to navigate swamps, these ungainly, wonderfully practical vessels compete in races that are telecast nationwide.

Specifically: Naples Area Tourism Bureau, 813-262-6141.

39 Everglades à la Carte

A vast river of sawgrass, unpredictable and unforgiving, the Everglades' 2,200 square miles are one of America's most ecologically important, most fragile, and most stunning national parks. Yet the 'Glades don't lunge out at you like the glaciers, redwoods, buttes, and mountains of our western parks. They just lie there shimmering in the heat, daring you to discover the dramas that are played out minute by minute in its mangrove swamps and hardwood hammocks, waterways, and rookeries.

If you're willing to rough it, get a backcountry permit and hike or canoe your way to a distant campsite deep in the 'Glades. Although the permits are free, access to the backcountry is limited. It's here that the sense of privilege is greatest. You're alone with nature in a teeming wilderness with a rhythm all its own. Alligators, snakes, enormous flocks of birds, wild orchids, marsh rabbits, turtles, deer, black bear, raccoons, oppossum, strangler fig trees the size of mansions, armadillos, bald eagles, and dozens of other sightings surround you.

With luck you may see a bobcat or a very rare Florida panther. Other endangered species seen here include the Florida manatee, snail kite, Schaus swallowtail butterfly, and American crocodile. Add in some of the best fishing in the nation, streaky sunrises and blazing sunsets, and you have an unforgettable adventure weekend in America's third-largest national park.

It was in this tangled wilderness that the Seminole Indians, a tribe made up of runaway slaves and renegade Indians from various tribes, made their last stand against the U.S. Army. Only after you've wandered the amazing maze of waterways, cypress swamps, lakes, islands, and impenetrable masses of razor-edged vegetation can you understand how the Seminoles were able to raid white settlements and then melt back into the wilderness for decades.

Unless at least one of you is an experienced backcountry camper, confine your Everglades camping to one of the developed campgrounds at Flamingo or Long Pine Key. Or if you prefer not to camp at all, stay at the air-conditioned Flamingo Lodge. Take a motel room or cottage with kitchen, and enjoy the swimming pool and restaurant. From here take day trips by canoe, tram, airboat, car, rental bicycle, and on foot via boardwalks.

Picnic at Paurotis Pond, hike the trail at Pa-hay-okee, walk the Gumbo Limbo trail at Royal Station, and take the two-hour narrated tour of Shark Valley.

Another insider's view of the Everglades is yours when you rent a houseboat and lose yourselves for a long weekend in the endless miles of lakes and rivers. You'll have a window on the nature show from a comfortable, mobile base camp with cooking facilities, radio contact, real beds, hot and cold running water, and screens against the ferocious insects. No boating experience is required, but it's a big help if you know how to anchor and read a chart.

Whatever your accommodations or outdoors abilities, start at the visitors center for orientation programs, information, maps, and brochures. Then play by the rules, which must be rigid to protect this threatened resource.

Specifically: Write to the Everglades National Park District Ranger, Box V, West Palm Beach, FL 33402 for information about the many access points to the Everglades. To book a guided canoe or camping trip, call Florida Adventures Inc., 407-677-0655. Houseboats and lodgings are available at the Flamingo Lodge Marina and Outpost Resort, 305-253-2241 or 813-695-3101.

40 Coral Gables Goes Global

It was perfectly planned in the 1920s, an entire city that goes on still proving today the sense and civility of good urban planning. Now surrounded completely by Miami, yet a pocket apart from it, Coral Gables is a serene Spanish Colonial island in a sea of city streets. Entire blocks filled with architectural gems are set among green spaces and winding waterways, creating an air of eighteenth-century Havana.

Although it's only seven minutes from Miami International Airport and ten minutes from downtown Miami, Coral Gables is another world. It's a village of smart, small offices and international trade, galleries, boutiques, and more fine restaurants per square mile than anywhere this side of Manhattan. Discover it in a weekend; delight in it forever.

If you like small European-style hotels, stay at the romantic old-world Hotel Place St. Michel, a thirty-room jewel on the corner of Ponce de Leon Boulevard and Alcazar Avenue in the heart of the Gables. Each room is different; each abounds in cozy touches such as paddle fans and antique bedsteads. Continental breakfast—buttery croissants and thick fruit conserves—are always included in the tariff.

You may decide to spend the entire weekend in the hotel itself, lingering over aperitifs in the rooftop garden or at the piano bar, choosing take-out pâtés and baguettes in the Charcuterie, browsing the shops, and dining in the very French, glowingly intimate Restaurant St. Michel.

Or stroll the streets nearby to soak up the arty, European ambience. With a self-guided tour map in hand, take a twenty-mile scenic loop by car or bicycle through the grace and grandeur of Old Spain as interpreted by early Florida developers.

The first Friday of every month, Gables Gallery Night invites browsers to eighteen galleries. Everyone is in a festival mood, enjoying changing exhibitions, complimentary refreshments, and a free trolley that shuttles among all the sites. Latin American art is especially trendy now, but the galleries' wares range from contemporary Caribbean to European masterworks.

Reserve a day for a driving tour through stately gateways past plazas centered with fountains and into tree-lined avenues. Delve into individual international enclaves built in Chinese, French, and Dutch South African styles. The original homes are still meticulously groomed, just as their farsighted planners had intended in the 1920s. Stop to swim in the Venetian Pool, which was built from a coral quarry in 1923. It's now on the National Register of Historic Places.

Within a short walk of the St. Michel are more than a dozen outstanding restaurants. Many have a Spanish or Cuban touch, but there's also a good choice of Oriental, Northern Italian, Mediterranean, French, and Austrian dining. Two Sisters in the Hyatt Regency showcases New World cuisine; Yuca has been showered with national honors; the Biltmore Hotel, restored to its 1920s splendor, serves continental specialties alfresco or in a formal dining room.

Just south of downtown, Fairchild Tropical Garden is a botanical showplace in a moist, warm environment where tropical fruits, nuts, shrubs, and flowers thrive. The largest tropical botanical garden in the continental United States, it's perfect for pensive strolling among eighty-three acres of pathways, rain forest, palm glades, sunken gardens, twittering birds, and intoxicating scents. Also nearby is Matheson Hammock Park, a breezy place to sun or picnic bordering Biscayne Bay.

Specifically: Hotel Place St. Michel, 162 Alcazar Avenue, Coral Gables, FL 33134, 305-444-1666. For brochures on driving tours, shopping, dining, accommodations and attractions, contact the Development Department, City of Coral Gables, 550 Biltmore Way, Coral Gables, FL 33114, 305-460-5311.

41 Boca Beyond the Beach

Located just above the Gold Coast, Boca Raton (rah TONE) rarely makes it into guidebooks beyond a glowing mention of the landmark Boca Raton Hotel and Club. Yet the community, dead center in a corridor that provides a year-round calendar of cultural smash hits, is more than a pretty playground.

Fort Lauderdale to the south and West Palm Beach to the north doubled and redoubled in size, but Boca spurned industrial growth in favor of upscale housing and clean, high-tech businesses. It's the home of IBM, Florida Atlantic University, and some 70,000 folks who have come here to find the good life. With them came a demand for good theater and dance, ultramodern performing arts centers, and museums that can boast collections that are biggest, best, or both. The International Museum of Cartoon Art here (opening in 1996) is the largest and most important collection of editorial, magazine, and comic book art in the world.

From your hotel base in Boca, drive north to West Palm Beach, where the Kravits Center for the Performing Arts hosts such artists as the Bolshoi Ballet, Yo-Yo Ma, and Shirley MacLaine. Or hop on I-95 for a short ride south to Fort Lauderdale's Broward Center for the Performing Arts to see stars of the magnitude of Itzhak Perlman, Anne Murray, or Art Garfunkel. Each center has a variety of venues from small or experimental theater to the largest arena performances.

In Boca itself, the Caldwell Theater presents classic dramas, musicals, and comedies. Royal Palm Dinner Theater is one of the state's best. The historic Royal Poinciana Playhouse in Palm Beach stages Broadway hits starring famous artists. The Boca Ballet Theater Company performs a full-length story ballet each summer starring professional dancers. Boca appearances are also made by the Miami City

Ballet, one of the ten largest in the nation, and Ballet Florida, a professional dance company.

The eighty-five-member Boca Raton Symphonic Pops performs October through May; the Florida Philharmonic also performs in Boca Raton, often with well-known guest artists. Opera Antica presents a Baroque festival of antique operas starring singers from the Met. Three grand operas are produced each season at the Kravits Center by the Palm Beach Opera. The annual Palm Beach Invitational International Piano Competition attracts the best players from around the world.

The Boca Raton Museum of Art's permanent collection includes works by Klee, Matisse, Picasso, and other greats. Nearby in West Palm Beach, the Ann Norton Sculpture Gardens feature an impressive sculpture collection plus one of the largest collections of palms in the world. The Norton Gallery of Art here is one of the foremost art museums in the nation, especially esteemed for its French impressionist and post-impressionist masterpieces, as well as an outstanding Chinese collection.

At the Museum of Art in Fort Lauderdale, the collection of CoBrA art (Copenhagen-Brussels-Amsterdam school) is the largest in the Americas; so is its collection of works by American impressionist William Glackens. Its African, Oceanic, American Indian, and pre-Columbian artifacts are outstanding, and it has a fine collection of Egyptian antiquities.

Worth Avenue, Palm Beach's famous strip of ultra-exclusive shops, is the home of the Royal Palm Gallery featuring internationally known artists. A directory that lists the art and sculpture galleries of Boca Raton and the Palm Beaches fills thirty pages; a listing of members of the Broward County

Cultural Affairs Council fills a 182-page book. If there's a cultural weekend on your calendar, Boca Raton is the place.

The historic, five-star Boca Raton Hotel and Club reigns over the Boca beach like the queen she is. Like many resorts in southeast Florida, the Club straddles the Intracoastal Waterway, which means having it all: golf and a marina on the mainland plus a long stretch of ocean beach. Stay on either side and get back and forth free aboard the Club's own yacht. The resort has a choice of fine restaurants, fitness center, tennis, swimming pools, croquet, golf, lush grounds and gardens, and specialty shopping.

Specifically: Palm Beach County Convention and Visitors Bureau, 1555 Palm Beach Lakes Boulevard, West Palm Beach, FL 33401, 800-242-1774 or 407-471-3995; the Greater Fort Lauderdale CVB, 200 East Las Olas, Fort Lauderdale, FL 33301, 305-765-4466; the Boca Raton Chamber of Commerce, 1800 North Dixie Highway, Boca Raton, FL 33432, 407-395-4433. Request arts and culture schedules well in advance to allow time for ordering tickets and reserving accommodations. Boca Raton Hotel and Club reservations, 800-327-0101.

42 Deco Nights, Haute Couture Days

For years there was talk of bulldozing the entire mess. South Beach, the southern end of the island that includes Miami Beach, had become a dreary ghetto of retirement hotels and abandoned buildings. The old hotels of the 1930s and '40s along Ocean Drive were abandoned by vacationers for snazzier high-rise hotels built right on the beach farther north on Collins Avenue.

Just in time, imaginative young developers began to see the funky flair of the shabby, low-rise hotels of South Beach. The entire district was put on the National Register of Historic Places, and the race to restoration was on. Today it's an exciting, bohemian "strip" of smartly renovated hotels across from a wide, cinnamon sand beach.

Make this a weekend of schmoozing by night among the youthful models and international trendsetters who work South Beach, and shopping by day up the beach at the Bal Harbour Shops. They're Worth Avenue, Rodeo Drive, the 8th Arrondissement, and Savile Row rolled into one tropical oasis.

Rooms at most Deco hotels are small, the bathrooms are tiny by today's standards, and the furnishings are straight out of a Joan Crawford film. Yet it works. Your accommodations are a romantic movie set where you half expect to meet a young Sinatra or Barbara Stanwyck coming out of an antique elevator. Deft little touches make up for the smaller rooms: European bottled water, herb shampoos and soaps, fresh flowers, and enormous closets that were built for visitors who, in the old days, came for the entire winter.

Rates are in the moderate and high-moderate category, and they often include a European-style cold breakfast buffet of croissants, meats, cheese, yogurts, and fruit. During breakfast you'll overhear a group of young French tourists chattering over coffee in one corner while in another a German film crew switches from English to German and back as they discuss the day's schedule. An Asian businessman checks in with a dozen big boxes of Taiwan imports.

A middle-aged couple are reading the Spanish-language edition of the *Miami Herald*. Across the street on the wide beach, bronzed young joggers wend their way agilely around elderly Hasidic Jews in heavy frock coats. Under a chickee shelter on the sand, a bum awakes from a muscatel drunk and tries to focus as a cross-dresser in red sequins slinks by. It's this mix of mod and punk with the conventional that gives South Beach an ambience unlike any other.

Restaurants such as Chili Pepper, Cafe Milano, Larios, and Shabeen compete for a smart dinner crowd who dine late at a leisurely Latin pace. At Shabeen the specialties are Jamaican; Beacon's American Bistro is known for its crab cakes; authentic Cuban meals are hearty and budget priced at the Puerto Sagua; Cafe Milano does great seafood with an Italian flair. Nick's at the marina on Alton Road attracts a yachty crowd with its inspired menu; Joe's Stone Crab (closed in summer) is an institution.

Most European and American tourists come just for the sunny weather and the great beach. Commercial travelers come for the location handy to downtown shops and a mammoth civic complex that includes a convention center, the Bass Museum of Art, and a center for the performing arts. Yuppies come to hang out in smart sidewalk cafés, coffee shops, and discos. The area has a highly visible gay component as well as a number of drag queens who come here to make the scene. The mix is what one writer has called an American paella.

Bal Harbour, with its shops, is at the far north end of the

island. Take the bus or drive up Collins Avenue (A1A) until you start seeing the logos of the world's most revered merchants: Saks, Neiman Marcus, Bottega Veneta, F.A.O. Schwarz, Ungaro, Cartier, Lillie Rubin, Louis Vuitton, Mark Cross, Nina Ricci, Tiffany, Polo/Ralph Lauren, Brooks Brothers, and dozens more.

The Bal Harbour Shops are an architectural first. Opened in 1965, the complex is an emerald oasis rimmed with sea grapes and palms, screened from rushing street traffic. Signs are understated. Attendants in Bahamian gendarme dress and pith helmets patrol the parking areas to assist customers in any way necessary.

Spend the day browsing, lunching, window gazing, or shopping for that special item. Then get back to South Beach in time for sundowners at a sidewalk café, a memorable dinner in a candlelit boîte, and dancing into the wee hours.

Specifically: Greater Miami Convention and Visitors Bureau, 701 Brickell Avenue, Miami, FL 33131, 800-283-2707 or 305-539-3000. Request a list of Art Deco hotels on South Beach. Reach Bal Harbour Shops from the mainland on the Broad Causeway or by driving north from South Beach. Bal Harbour Tourism is at 655 96th Street, Bal Harbour, FL 33154, 305-573-5177 or 800-847-9222.

43 Islands in the Stream
Dry Tortugas

Many of Florida's islands are covered in another of our books, *Florida Under Sail* (Country Roads Press). If you love islands, the two of you can vacation on a different Florida island every month for years without running out of new ones to call your own. Some can be reached by road, some only by boat, but all are special in some way. Most couples eventually begin talking about "our" Sanibel or "our" Indian River Plantation.

Superlatives fail when it comes to the Dry Tortugas, which are different from all the rest. Far out to sea, seventy miles from Key West, the Tortugas are beyond the reach of speedboaters who buzz casually into other islands for a quick afternoon picnic. To camp here requires planning and supplies and, when you arrive, there are no creature comforts except for those you bring along. You'll arrive by seaplane, offload your gear, and be picked up again at a prearranged date.

Is it worth it? Yes! Because there are no rivers to carry silt into the ocean, the waters here are as clear as gin. Snorkel with visibility unlimited in an underwater wildlife sanctuary that abounds with sea life. Lobsters, safe from fishermen's spears, grow to monster size, and the brilliant reef fish flash like gemstones in the sunlit waters.

On land, another wildlife show goes on. Because this sprinkling of islands is the only resting place for miles around during spring and fall migrations between the northern states and Latin America, migratory birds arrive in huge, fluttering flocks of color and song. Bush Key hosts some of the largest colonies of sooty and noddy terns in the world. Boobies, frigate birds, and 150 other varieties from large seabirds to small songbirds put on a daily show during migration seasons.

Dive among the coral reefs

To crown it all, Garden Key is the home of Fort Jefferson, the largest masonry structure in the Western Hemisphere. Walls fifty feet high and eight feet thick are made of 16 million bricks. Work went on for almost thirty years before the project was abandoned because leaking cisterns made it impossible to supply the garrison with adequate water. Besides, the invention of rifled cannon, which could shoot right through brick walls, made this fort militarily untenable.

It was here that Dr. Samuel Mudd was imprisoned as a suspected Lincoln assassination conspirator. A country doctor, he had set a broken leg. Unfortunately for him, the patient was John Wilkes Booth. Mudd was released for his heroism in treating yellow fever victims at the fort, and eventually his name was cleared. Fort Jefferson's next moment in history came at the turn of the century, when the battleship *Maine* took on coal here for the voyage to Cuba. When she was blown up in Havana Harbor, "Remember the Maine" became a rallying cry in the Spanish-American War. Visitors are free to roam the fort's long corridors and cool dungeons.

Full- and half-day round-trip seaplane excursions are available. En route, you'll fly over the Marquesa Keys, a true coral atoll, and you'll see the large white-sand area known as Quicksands. Look down on the wreck sights that made Mel Fisher famous, and fly low over schools of manta rays twirling a graceful ballet. Arrange to stop briefly to snorkel and see the fort, and return to Key West.

To make the Dry Tortugas truly your own, however, camp here overnight. Park regulations allow stays of up to fourteen days, but it's rugged duty and most campers stay only two or three days. You'll be marooned under the stars, with nothing more than can be stuffed into one small backpack.

The only facilities on the island are rest rooms with no showers, and one drinking water fountain that supplies purified rainwater. No stoves or combustibles are allowed. Cooking is done on self-lighting charcoal. No dive tanks can be brought; no trash can be left. Everything must be brought back with you to Key West. You can, however, arrange for the seaplane to resupply you with ice as well as with any other supplies you leave behind with the air service.

Specifically: Make reservations well ahead of time with Key West Seaplane Service, 305-294-6978 or 800-224-2359. For camping, a minimum stay of two nights is recommended. All food, supplies, and camping gear, including fresh water, must be brought with you; luggage is limited to forty pounds.

If you don't care to camp on the island, take a round-trip sightseeing flight that stops long enough for a quick look and a dip in the ocean.

Orland-based Central Reservation Service also has a Miami office. Through them, hotels and rental cars can be booked in Florida and nationwide. Call 800-950-0232 or 800-226-4866. In Canada, call 800-950-0232.

44 Where Is Aventura?

Although it is a little-known mailing address, this community between Fort Lauderdale and Miami is home to some of the swankiest resorts, condos, and shops in the state. Seductive, cosmopolitan, and a sleek hideaway only minutes off one of the state's busiest interstates, Turnberry Isle Resort and Club is nestled along the Intracoastal Waterway with easy access, via free shuttle, to its own private ocean beach and marina.

A Rafael hotel and a member of Leading Hotels of the World, the resort sprawls over 300 tropical acres. For solitude, lose yourself in the lush gardens or charter a boat to take just the two of you offshore for fishing or sunset watching. Have room service bring breakfast to your suite or serve a sumptuous champagne supper overlooking gardens and lakes. Steal away to the beach just before dawn and watch the sun lift out of the Atlantic.

When you want company, join the fun at the twenty-four lighted tennis courts, four swimming pools, a half dozen indoor and outdoor restaurants, a spa, and a daily calendar of planned events.

Live entertainers play the restaurants and lounges; activities staff plan special mixers several days a week. You might plug into a group trip to a hockey game at the Miami Arena, a toga party at the spa, a special happy hour on St. Patrick's Day, or Prime Rib Night at the Monaco Restaurant.

Florida is famous for its landmark golf resorts, each noted for one or more features that are heralded throughout the golfing world. At Turnberry Isle, which has two Robert Trent Jones–designed championship golf courses, it's the Island Green. It really *is* an island. Lake Julius, named for golfer Julius Boros, who lives nearby, comes into direct play on nine of the eighteen holes of the challenging South Course and edges three more holes.

Tennis greats including John McEnroe, Bjorn Borg, Jimmy Connors, and Vitas Gerulaitis trained at Turnberry Isle. Tennis Hall of Famer and former Wimbledon champion Fred Stolle is resident pro. Televised tournaments played here have featured Martina Navratilova and Jimmy Connors. Play on clay or hard courts, and keep one eye out for celebrities.

Spa goers will enjoy the zesty, fresh approach at Turnberry's spa. The accent here is not on the quick fix, but on sending each guest home with a new regimen based on his or her own lifestyle. De-stress is the keyword here in classes ranging from yoga and aerobics to rollerblading. Special exercise classes are designed for golfers, joggers, and tennis players. Entire rooms are filled with Nautilus and Cybex stations.

What sets most of south Florida apart from the rest of the state is the exotic, cosmopolitan makeup of the guest list at the best resorts. At Turnberry, the continental mix adds to the tony ambience. Wealthy Europeans come for winter vacations; South Americans come in summer to escape their own winter. Businesspersons from Miami mingle with leisure guests from the Northeast; serious golfers and tennis players meet tyros who come here for instruction from famous professionals; ordinary people rub elbows with famous names who come for pampering at the spa. It's a recipe for a weekend to remember.

Specifically: Turnberry Isle Resort and Club, 19999 West Country Club Drive, Aventura, FL 33180, 305-932-6200 or 800-233-1588. Flying in, the resort is equally handy to both FLL and MIA. Ask about honeymoon, golf, or tennis packages.

45 Doral Golf Resort and Spa
Miami

If the name sounds familiar, it's because this is the landmark resort where the televised Doral-Ryder Open is played, where Arthur Ashe was tennis pro for more than twenty years, and where famous personalities come for very private pampering in one of the nation's great spas. Here's one weekend where you can have it all—his, hers, and ours.

Under new management and on fast-track renovation since 1994, the Doral has become one of Florida's prestige addresses, splayed across 650 acres of sun-splashed statuary and greenery. It's inland, only ten minutes from Miami International Airport. Rooms here are what most hotels call junior suites, complete with mini-bar, sitting room, and enormous bathroom. If you upgrade to one of the spacious suites at the ultra-posh Spa, your suite is even more regal. The bathrooms alone are larger than most hotel rooms, and the decor in each suite is different.

If you're golfers, play the famous Blue Monster course or the resort's other challenging courses. The Doral has eighty-one holes to choose from. Take instruction at the Golf Learning Center under the direction of PGA Master Pro Jim McLean. Whatever your skill level, from beginner to master, you'll get the latest in high-tech training complete with video analysis of your game, weight and balance breakdown of your swing, and even a device that measures the speed of your drive.

If you prefer, sign on for a tennis package and private lessons with tennis professionals or the tennis director. Choose from fifteen courts day or night, and let the resort match you up with a partner if your own partner deserts you for the golf course or spa. The advantage of a resort like this is that you can do everything together or go your separate ways for a few hours, meet for lunch, then do an activity that you enjoy together.

For a simple, lazy weekend, take the Classic Getaway for Two, which includes accommodations, champagne, breakfast in bed, and a candlelight dinner in your room. Add any golf, tennis, or spa services à la carte, or simply hang out at the pool and sit under the thundering mineral cascade waterfalls. Dine in the spa dining room, the grill, or the gourmet restaurant, Windows.

If you drive in, park the car for the weekend and forget it. If you fly in, the Doral will pick you up at the airport. Inside these verdant acres, the outside world of jangling traffic seems miles away.

For the most sensuous of weekends, take one of the packages offered by the Spa at the Doral. Included in the Grand Getaway for Two are a deluxe room, three spa meals daily, and meltingly luxurious treatment in the hands of a talented spa staff. Take your choice of services: massage, aromatherapy, herbal wrap, cleansing and de-stress facials, and much more.

Use any of the spa's other facilities too: fitness classes on all skill levels, boxer aerobics, a high-tech equipment room, whirlpool, sauna, steam room, cooking and nutrition classes, private balconies for sunning, and an indoor jogging track.

Spa wellness coordinators, beauticians, and technicians shop the world for the most exotic lotions, minerals, muds, oils, and treatments. Let them use the treatments on you, and teach you how to use them on yourself or each other. An entire shop is devoted to these divine products, many of them formulated exclusively for the Spa at the Doral.

Specifically: Doral Golf Resort and Spa is at 4400 N.W. 87th Avenue, Miami, FL 33178, 305-593-6030. Reservations, 800-331-7768. Prices are in the luxury range; packages are the best value. Rates are lowest June through mid-December.

46 Catch Conch Fever
Key West

Key West is different from the rest of Florida, even from the rest of the Keys. Good travel writers don't use the cliché "city of contrasts," but this is it. Key West is maverick, yet prissy; upscale, yet slummy; eccentric, even zany.

It's touristy to the max, yet nowhere else can you find so many pockets of privacy. To locals, Live and Let Live is a religion. Its residents are independent to the point of lunacy, yet they can behave like lemmings when it comes to preserving their own fiefdom, their Conch Republic. It's Margaritaville, and anything goes.

Getting here is half the fun. Drive the Overseas Highway, scenic and slow, in about three hours from Miami. Come in by commuter plane or on one of the cruise ships that call here for a day. Or take a weekend package aboard a Vintage Air Tours DC-3 out of Kissimmee or Fort Lauderdale. Big-band music plays on the plane's loudspeaker, stewardesses wear 1940s uniforms, and service harks back to the good ol' days when air travel was rakish and elite.

Although Key West burned before the turn of the century and has been knocked flat in hurricanes as recently as the 1930s, it has many surviving historic homes, including some of the most opulent Victorian mansions in the South. Entire homes were assembled in the Bahamas and brought here by ship long before the island was connected to the mainland in 1912. At one time, long before Miami emerged as a major player, Key West's waterfront was the busiest port between Nassau and New Orleans.

Ships that foundered on nearby reefs were picked clean by professional wreckers who furnished their Key West homes with the best goods from all over the world. In one census, it was the richest community in America. By the 1930s, it was the poorest.

Make your weekend as relaxing, brainless, active, or intellectual as you wish. Shop for hand-printed fabrics, hand-made sandals and jewelry, and locally made perfumes, or hunt bargains at Fast Buck Freddy's. Haunt art museums and galleries. Take a hike into history at Harry Truman's winter White House and the restored nineteenth-century lighthouse and keeper's quarters. See the home where Ernest Hemingway wrote *For Whom the Bell Tolls* and *A Farewell to Arms*, and the house where Audubon came to paint birds.

Come on an ordinary weekend or during one of the year's many festivals. Stay in one of the many historic inns such as the Artist House (1890), Curry Mansion (1899), Duval House (1880), Key West Bed and Breakfast (the Russell House, circa 1898), or The Marquesa (1884). Or choose a fine, full-service hotel such as the Hyatt, Pier House, The Reach, or Marriott's historic Casa Marina. Key West also has popular chain motels as well as specialty accommodations catering to gays or vegetarians.

For the ultimate in resort luxury, stay at Little Palm Island, once an exclusive fish camp for Harry Truman and his cronies and later the scene of the film *PT-109*. It's twenty-eight miles north of Key West off Little Torch Key. As close to a South Pacific paradise as can be found in the Keys, it's rimmed with palm trees and reached only by boat. Prices are in the $500/night range plus the mandatory meal plan, but the luxuries and service are impressive. You'll have your own thatch-roofed villa in a setting of lonely beaches, a heated pool, a busy marina, gift shop, masseuse, the use of sailboats and other watercraft, and meals that give new meaning to the term gourmet.

Dining in Key West is as eclectic as the city itself. Shorty's Diner still serves its Harry's Special breakfast, the same menu Harry Truman ordered (eggs, pancakes, bacon) every day. Pepe's has long served a complete Thanksgiving dinner every Thursday, for under $10. Louie's Backyard is one of several gourmet restaurants that have caught national notice; other excellent dining can be found in the better hotels.

The Conch Train and Old Town Trolley are still the best way to begin every visit to Key West. Take one or both of these tours to get oriented, then pick up a free Pelican Path map at the tourist center at Mallory Square and take off on foot. Key West is for walking or bicycling; driving is difficult and parking is impossible.

End your days back at Mallory Square, arriving an hour before sunset. Here Sunset is a nightly ritual complete with buskers, massage artists, religious zealots, soapbox speakers, vendors, and hucksters, with the backdrop of a truly gorgeous sunset.

Each year, two million tourists do what in the Keys is called to "go all the way" (to Key West). Of them, 85 percent will return time and again for the madness and magic of this maverick island.

Specifically: Chamber of Commerce, P.O. Box 984, Key West, FL 33040, 800-LAST KEY or 305-294-2587. Request maps, brochures, lists of accommodations and restaurants. Vintage Air Tours, 407-932-1400. Little Palm Island, 800-343-8567 or 305-872-2524.

142

47 Moon Over Miami

It's at the end of the road, the perfect place to heal after an imperfect workweek. Fly or drive into Miami and feel the world's cares fall away as you motor out of the city and over the causeway onto the island of Key Biscayne. Since time began, the sea has been scrubbing clean the sands of Biscayne's beaches with each new tide. What better spot for new beginnings together than this convenient paradise in the shadow of a crowded city?

A popular travel magazine named the beaches here among the nation's top ten. Dangling at the end of a long string of barrier islands that straggle down Florida's east coast from Jacksonville Beach to Miami Beach, Key Biscayne looks east onto the unbroken Atlantic and west across the vast expanse of Biscayne Bay. Don't be confused by addresses. Dozens of mainland sites and an entire national park claim Biscayne Bay. It's *Key* Biscayne, with its ocean beaches and exclusive resorts, that make this weekend.

At the 300-room Sonesta Beach Resort, check into a king- or queen-size room with a balcony overlooking the ocean. Dine at your choice of the resort's three restaurants, then retire to Desires for dancing and listening. For a more pubby atmosphere, hang out in the lounge's alcove for billiards and darts. Or order from the twenty-four-hour room service and have dinner for two on your balcony.

The Links of Key Biscayne are a challenging, seventy-two-hole championship public course, home of the Royal Caribbean Senior PGA Golf Classic. It's two miles from the resort. Or stay on the grounds to enjoy the three-mile beach, water sports, a sports court with basketball and roller skating, nine tennis courts, shops, and jewelry classes.

Order a box lunch, rent a bicycle, and spend one of your

Miami's famed Art Deco style

days exploring the island. Crandon Park, with its gardens and walking paths, lies at the north end. To the south is Bill Baggs Cape Florida State Park. Both have dazzling public beaches, alight with graceful gulls.

Bike all the way to the southern tip of the key to see the romantic Cape Florida Lighthouse, which has an exciting history that park rangers will tell you about. In a setting of seaside and lush greenery, it's one of the prettiest parks in the state. Watch for bitterns, limpkin, roseate spoonbills, anhingas, tropical songbirds, and seabirds of all sizes.

For centuries, the Gulf Stream off this island was a trade route for merchants and pirates. The fast-flowing Stream added a bonus of about four knots to wind-driven ships, speeding their way from Havana to St. Augustine. It was near here in 1733 that fourteen ships of the Spanish Plate fleet wrecked on the reefs during a hurricane. Only one survived. Some of the treasure is sure to be covered by these sands. At least it's fun to think so as you slosh barefoot through warm surf, hand in hand, looking for pieces of eight.

Specifically: Greater Miami Convention and Visitors Bureau, 701 Brickell Avenue, #2700, Miami, FL 33131, 800-283-2707 or 305-539-3063. Sonesta Beach Resort, 350 Ocean Drive, Key Biscayne, FL 33149, 305-361-2021. Also on the island are a Sheraton, 305-361-5775, and the Key Islander Executive Suites, 305-361-2464.

48 The Islands of Pine Island Sound

A pocket of placid green water shimmers in the Gulf of Mexico off Fort Myers, protected by Sanibel and Captiva to the west and Pine Island to the east. Every guidebook lists Sanibel and Captiva, and for good reason. They're remote, yet reachable by road, and developed to the point where they offer an attractive variety of accommodations, shopping, nature trails, beaches, restaurants, and recreation.

After the end of the road, however, the islands straggle on ever farther out to sea. One of the more famous is Cabbage Key, where mystery writer Mary Roberts Rinehart built an inn in the 1930s. It's a favorite stop for excursion boats and private yachts that put in for a meal at the ramshackle restaurant. The evening atmosphere is pubby, with darts and perhaps someone pounding the upright piano. For overnighters there are a few guest rooms or cottages.

Even if you're staying on the mainland or on one of the drive-to islands, reserve a day for cruising the islands of Pine Island Sound. Some are privately owned; some are mere sandbars where shelling is unequaled.

We first heard about Useppa Island in the 1970s when it was being restored as an exclusive community. Thought to be named for Joseffa, a mistress of pirate Jose Gaspar, the island was home to Calusa Indians as early as 5000 B.C. It was purchased in 1912 by wealthy northerners and developed as the ultra-exclusive Izaak Walton Anglers Club, where Tiffany diamond stickpins were awarded when a member caught a record tarpon.

An illegal casino hummed through elegant evenings while daytimes found residents playing chess with life-size pieces, swimming in the pool, playing the golf course, or sailing off the sandy beaches. The club had its own fine dining, library, water and electrical systems, and a grand social season that attracted such guests as Teddy Roosevelt, Mae West, the Mellons, and the DuPonts.

In time, fickle guests made their winter homes elsewhere. Elegant cottages, abandoned to the sun and rains, were invaded by rats and raccoons. Intruding rains rotted oak floors; wind-lashed debris smashed through delicate windowpanes. Vines devoured the delicate white trellises that are the island's trademark.

When new owners began a rescue operation in the 1970s, some cottages couldn't be saved. Today, however, it's hard to guess which structures are new and which were built in the millionaire era. The island with its spiffy white homes, bright beveled glass, and wide verandas has the feel of a turn-of-the-century village. Everything is easily reached on the wide footpaths through a botanical treasure trove of trees and shrubs that have been brought here from all over the world. No cars are in evidence.

Suites, cottages, and villas with up to four bedrooms can be rented by the day or week. Or come in your boat and dock at the marina for the night, dining at the Barron Collier Room (jackets after 6:00 P.M.) and breakfasting in the friendly, informal Izaak Walton Club Grille. Don't miss the bar, where thousands of shiny tarpon scales are enshrined in casting resin. They remain from the original club, when it was not yet known that taking a scale from a tarpon would probably result in its death. Today, tarpon fishing is still a local passion but catches are released swiftly and gently.

Useppa's ambience remains that of a tight little island. Still a private club, it's aloof from the world but offers a friendly welcome to those guests who venture here. Walk anywhere in five minutes, from the clubby public areas or the excellent little museum, to remote beaches, to the dockside gazebo where locals like to congregate to watch the sunset.

Specifically: Useppa Island Club, Box 640, Bokeelia, FL 33922, 813-283-1061. For area information, Lee County Visitor and Convention Bureau, 2180 West First Street, Fort Myers, FL 33902, 813-338-3500. Ask about excursion or rental boats and ferry information. Scheduled ferries serve Useppa Island. *Lady Chadwick*, which sails out of South Seas Plantation, Box 194, Captiva, FL 33924, 813-472-7549, offers lunch stops at your choice of the two islands. Reservations are a must for accommodations, transportation, dock space, and meals in the islands.

49 A Looney Tunes™ Weekend

While many ships run weekend cruises out of Florida ports, the Big Red Boats of Premier Cruise Lines offer just the right blend of luxury and informality, couples and families, and a touch of whimsy because Bugs Bunny, Tweetie Bird, Sylvester, and all the other Looney Tunes characters are on board.

Play it your way. At the top of the price scale are spacious suites and apartment suites. For half their price, you can get a small stateroom with bunk beds. The best mid-price compromise is a double- or queen-bed cabin on a middle deck.

If you're new to cruising, remember that, except for your cabin size, it's classless. Every passenger gets the same dazzling musical extravaganzas, lavish meals, and eye-popping midnight buffet nightly, a choice of lounges with live music and dancing, and VIP service from an attentive European staff. If you bring the children, they'll have their own nonstop carousel of daytime fun. Round-the-clock child care is also available on Premier ships.

Before you sail from Port Canaveral, the Welcome Aboard buffet is already beckoning. It's the first of six meals daily, not counting snacks, tea parties, room service, and make-your-own-sundae parties.

Unpack and you're "home" and yet mobile. Wake up the next morning in Nassau, where you can stay onboard for a day-long schedule of fun. Or go ashore to sail through coral reefs on a real submarine, learn to scuba, take a glass-bottom boat tour, explore the historic city of Nassau with or without guides, or spend the day on an uninhabited, uninhibited private island. Here you can laze in a hammock strung between coconut palms, swim or board-sail off five beaches in water as clear as Perrier, or get up a game of volleyball. Go back to the ship for dinner and a show or dancing. Or take another shore tour to the Las Vegas–style Crystal Palace Casino Show, a native calypso evening, or a moonlight cruise of Nassau Harbor.

If you're still hungry when you get back to the ship in the wee hours, there's Insomnia Service or twenty-four-hour room service. Sleep well while the ship's crew stand watch. You'll wake up in Port Lucaya on exciting Grand Bahama Island, as modern as Nassau is ancient. The ship's own upbeat tempo continues to throb for those who choose to stay onboard. On shore, choose the glass-bottom boat tour, Dolphin Encounter, eighteen holes of golf, scuba diving or lessons, snorkeling, a tour of the island's historical highlights, or parasailing.

Cruising, which has become one of America's most popular vacations, has gained a loyal following because it offers a feeling of total getaway with all the pleasures and comforts of a five-star resort. Aboard ship you can party around the clock, join the nonstop action poolside, or seek out a quiet deck where the two of you can be alone. If you want to pursue separate interests, one of you can play bridge while the other joins a trivia game. Then meet for a drink in the Big Chill and dance to '50s music before dinner.

Dine on continental cuisine, pizza, or the low-fat spa selections. Enjoy sit-down dining at linen-covered tables or choose one of the buffets. There may be a country barbecue on deck with line dancing. Or a Mexican feast with conga and limbo. Take your chances in the Casino. Join the group who are playing Family Feud. Go to a movie. Try Karaoke.

Just to read the brochure can leave the prospective passenger breathless and perhaps even skeptical. You may have to try a weekend afloat to believe it. Aboard the Big Red Boat, you'll discover all the good things that are offered by longer and more expensive cruises all crammed into a quick but unbelievably refreshing weekend.

Specifically: The Big Red Boats of Premier Cruise Lines are booked only through travel agents. Ask yours for a brochure, then decide on the package that is right for you.

50 One in Ten Thousand
Marco Island

On southwest Florida's Gulf coast, the mainland doesn't just stop at the sea. It peters out into marshes, swamps, and then into the constellation of sandbars, mangroves, and islets known as the Ten Thousand Islands. Only one is inhabited. It's Marco Island, the end of the road for travelers driving west from Miami or south from Naples.

Calusa Indians, the last of tribes that are known to have inhabited this cay for about 3,500 years, called it Caxambas, meaning fresh water. They settled here and began building it ever higher with shell mounds that today rise as much as fifty feet above sea level. In piling the daily trash of generations, they deposited a treasury of archaeological finds. Fiber-tempered pottery dated at 1450 B.C. has been dug up; some fragments were pegged as early as 3015 B.C.

Long a sleepy fishing outpost plagued with rattlesnakes, Marco Island came awake to the sweet kiss of developers' dollars after a causeway was built to the mainland. The snakes were cleaned out, and suddenly Marco has a snazzy style to complement its sandy beaches and turquoise waters. Along the Gulf, a fringe of fancy hotels includes a four-star, four-diamond Hilton, a Marriott resort and golf club, and a Radisson resort built in Art Deco style.

For utter escape you can't fault the lazy pace, a climate that almost always promises warm sun in the dead of winter, and good restaurants galore. All of Marco's recreational roads lead back to the sea. The island is only four by six miles, with a four-mile sandbox beach. Some people do nothing more than stroll the surf line, sunning and shelling, and splashing into the Gulf for an occasional cooldown. Or rent a water bike, board sailer, or spiffy little sailboat from your hotel.

Launch your own boat at the public ramp, or rent a boat

with or without a guide. Charter a sportfishing boat. Canoe among the uninhabited mangrove islands, or book a sightseeing or sunset cruise.

Take a shelling expedition to offshore sandspits and a swamp buggy tour of the Everglades. Tee off on your choice of forty area golf courses set among tropical hammocks and shining lagoons. Shop the galleries and specialty boutiques, or hunt bargains at a thirty-store factory outlet.

The larger resorts have activities directors and a large menu of aerobics, tennis mixers, cooking classes, bingo, and other group fun to share with travelers who flock here from England, Canada, Germany, and the United States. Or simply sit on your balcony overlooking the Gulf to watch the nightly spectacle of the sun melting into the water.

For orientation, start with the chatty, comfortable trolley tour. If you want to shop or eat, get off this trolley and catch the next one. They run all day. Dining choices abound. Larger hotels have up to half a dozen restaurants each, and there are probably another half dozen eateries within walking distance of your home hotel.

If you're history buffs, take a self-guided island tour identified by limestone markers at each stop. By car or bicycle, start at the end of the toll bridge and note the marker at a 3,500-year-old archaeological site. Other historic points are the landing for the ferries that brought traffic to the island until 1938, the schoolhouse built in 1889, and the old settlers' cemetery. Around the island, Calusa mounds and other old sites are also marked.

The Goodland Fish House in the island's historic fishing village is a scene straight out of the film *Key Largo*; so is the Snook Inn in Old Marco. Dinner and dancing at the century-old Old Marco Inn is a visit to a sweet Victorian yesterday.

The entire island is a protected wildlife sanctuary. Watch

153

A young alligator taking the sun

for West Indian manatees, giant loggerhead turtles, and bald eagles. Collect a bucketful of horse conchs, whelks, lions' paws, and Scotch bonnets. Touring nearby preserves, you may see an Everglades mink or a rare Florida panther.

Marco Island may be at land's end, but it's also the entry to one of the state's richest nature shows.

Specifically: Chamber of Commerce, 1102 South Collier Boulevard, Marco Island, FL 33937, 800-788-MARCO or 813-394-7549.

51 Sunny Sunday Jazz Brunch
Fort Lauderdale

If you still remember Fort Lauderdale as the teenage skin-flick mecca of the 1970s, it's time to schedule another trip. Parking has been moved back from what is still one of the best stretches of brown-sugar beach in the Sunshine State. The congestion along the shore has been eliminated, and shuttle service from the remote parking areas is free. Bring a blanket, a cooler, sun block, and stale bread to feed flashing seagulls that can churn a beautiful seascape into a stunning work of motion sculpture. The combination of creamy surf, sand, sunshine, and this ballet of birds is unforgettable.

Local promotions are no longer aimed at a beer-budget spring-break crowd, and a new sophistication has settled over a city that sparkles with shiny new stuff. The biggest shows and name entertainers play the Performing Arts Center, which is next to the Riverwalk site of the jazz brunch. Local restaurants and resorts are world class. The annual boat parade, Las Olas art show, and Bahia Mar boat show are destination events that bring visitors from all over the country.

A Sunday staple along the new Riverwalk is the gala jazz brunch, held the first Sunday of every month. Couples cluster around four stages set up along the river, to listen to cool jazz from 11:00 A.M. to 2:00 P.M. Some of the city's best restaurants are also on hand to serve brunch alfresco. The jazz is hot, fresh, and free.

The monthly event takes on the look of a street festival with face painting, artists offering to sketch your caricature, exotic birds, and other displays. Bring your camera, come early, and don't leave until the last lick.

The rest of your weekend can be spent at the beach, shopping antique row in Dania or the mammoth Sawgrass Outlet Mall, sportfishing, scuba diving, or sightseeing. Start your visit with a ninety-minute tour on Lolly the Trolley, a Fort Lauderdale institution. Buy an all-day pass; the trolley stops at points of interest and you can get off and on at your own pace, getting acquainted with the one-way traffic mazes before you set out on your own.

The *Jungle Queen*, another venerable Fort Lauderdale fixture, still steams twice a day out of Bahia Mar Yacht Basin. The gossipy narration is great fun, and the nightly barbecue dinner cruises are a belly-busting feast complete with sing-alongs and corny humor.

The International Swimming Hall of Fame has memorabilia honoring great names in swimming history. Visitors can also swim laps in the two Olympic pools. If you're a serious student of swimming history, take advantage of the library, films, and videos too.

The city has two other notable museums: the Museum of Art, which has some outstanding collections of modern and classic works, and the Museum of Discovery and Science, which has an IMAX theater. Parker Playhouse, located in Holiday Park, offers professional theater November through May. The eighty-six-acre park itself is open all year for tennis, swimming, and picknicking.

Historic homes along the river include that of early settler Frank Stranahan. He set up a trading post for Seminole Indians who left their reservation up the river and came into Fort Lauderdale for supplies. When his wife realized that most of them couldn't read, she founded a school for them. A beloved local pioneer, she lived on in this house long after her husband died. It's now preserved as a museum, giving visitors a view of how people lived only a few years ago when Fort Lauderdale was a remote outpost on the edge of the dark, forbidding Everglades.

Specifically: Call 305-761-5363 for a recorded list of this month's jazz and other events sponsored by the local parks and recreation department. For lists of accommodations and sightseeing, contact the Convention and Visitors Bureau, 200 East Las Olas Boulevard, Fort Lauderdale, FL 33301, 305-765-4466.

52 Happy Trails to You

Florida is threaded with ancient, pre-Columbian trails, some forested and some liquid, but all of them still wildly beautiful. When the two of you want a challenging weekend in the rugged outdoors, away from the crush that seems to cover all of south Florida in winter, here are some trails that take you away from the crowds.

Bike the Keys is a two-day, 101-mile route from the Chekika Ranger Station in Everglades National Park to John Pennekamp Coral Reef State Park on Key Largo. If you have time for a layover, you can also take a ranger-led canoe trek through Pennekamp. The bicycle route is on public roads shared with automobiles.

The Lake Okeechobee Trail circles the lake, linking four sections of the Florida trail in segments that are twenty to thirty-six miles long. The path follows the dike, so you can't always see the lake itself through dense vegetation, but the natural sightseeing is sublime. The route takes you through a land of lakes, rivers, natural springs, hardwood forests, and hammocks. Pause often to listen for birdsongs, smell the wildflowers, and sweep the surroundings for the wildlife that is watching you.

DuPuis Reserve State Forest's wet prairie, cypress marshes, and pine flatwoods surround four hiking and backpacking trails that are from 4.3 to 15.5 miles long. A connecting trail takes you into an adjacent wildlife management area. Trails are also available for horseback riding and bicycling.

Fern Forest is a 354-acre oasis of native plants in the heart of heavily populated Pompano Beach. Hike through colorful swamp maples and hardwoods, counting up to thirty-two species of moist, green ferns.

Hungryland Boardwalk through the slash pine woods and sawgrass marsh west of Palm Beach Gardens is only 1.2 miles long, but it's here that you can enter a fourteen-mile spur of the Florida Trail through a 60,000-acre wildlife management area. Take the short trail through a cypress wetland filled with ferns and air plants, or opt for the longer trek across flatwoods, marshes, and hardwood forests.

Jonathan Dickinson State Park is known mostly for its ranger-guided boat tours, but for those who want to venture far into the park there are canoe, bicycle, and horse trails. One of the hiking trails is a 9.3-mile section of the Florida Trail. The park, which has cabin rentals, is a good place to headquarter for the weekend.

Long Key State Recreation Area is a shining marine morass where you can take canoe trails through tidal, saltwater lakes or hike nature trails that are high and dry. An easier walk is across the lagoon by boardwalk. Most visitors cluster at the fabulous beaches, leaving the trails to you. Tenting, swimming, boating, and nature viewing are superb. See if you can spot a tiny Key deer.

Loxahatchee National Wildlife Refuge is only ten miles west of bustling Boynton Beach, yet its trails through the wilderness of the northern Everglades take you back almost to the dinosaur age. Try the two easy, interpreted short trails or longer canoe or dike trails.

Treetops Park, tucked into urban Davie, is named for its towering oaks. Take the canoe or horseback trails.

West Lake Park, at 1,400 acres, is one of the largest urban parks in the state. Hike, bicycle, or paddle along trails through mangrove wetlands that rustle with birdlife. The tangled roots of the mangroves form a marine nursery that is one of nature's richest gifts to the sea. It's in Oakland Park, between Fort Lauderdale and Pompano Beach.

159

Specifically: Request the booklet *Florida Trails* from the Division of Tourism, 107 West Gaines Street, Suite 558, Tallahassee, FL 32399, 904-487-1462. Listed by region are the state's scenic trails on land and water. Florida Trail Association, Box 13708, Gainesville, FL 32604, 352-378-8823, or 800-343-1882, has as its goal the completion of 1,300 miles of continuous hiking trails throughout the state.

Index

AIR STATIONS, FLYING
  Fighter piloting, 106–107
  Fighter Pilots USA, 107
  Mayport Naval Air Station,
    Mayport, 86
ALHAMBRA DINNER
    THEATER, Jacksonville,
    86
ANIMALS. *See also* WILDLIFE
    REFUGES
  Busch Gardens, Tampa,
    16–17
  Conservancy Nature Center,
    Naples, 118
  Java Monkeys, Miami, 111
  Lowry Park Zoo, Tampa, 90
  Manatees, Blue Springs,
    88–90
  Sea World, Orlando, 89–90
ARCHITECTURE
  Apalachicola, 81
  Belleview Mido, Clearwater,
    10–11
  Coral Gables, 122
  North Hill Preservation
    District, Pensacola, 70
  Palafox District, Pensacola,
    70
  Stouffer Vinoy, St.
    Petersburg, 11
  Stuart Feed Supply, Stuart, 8
  South Beach, 128

  St. Nicholas Greek
    Orthodox Church,
    Tarpon Springs, 20
ART MUSEUMS/GALLERIES
  Appleton Museum of Art,
    25
  Boca Raton International
    Museum of Cartoon Art,
    94
  Boca Raton Museum of Art,
    Boca Raton, 126
  Clewiston, 2
  Cummer Gallery of Art,
    Jacksonville, 86
  DeSoto Museum, 29
  Don Garlitz Museum of
    Drag Racing, 25
  Florida International
    Museum, 11
  Florida Museum of Natural
    History, Gainesville,
    78
  Gables Gallery Night, Coral
    Gables, 123
  George Inness Sr.
    Universalist Church,
    Tarpon Springs, 20
  International Museum of
    Cartoon Art, Boca Raton,
    125
  Jacksonville Art Museum,
    86

Karpeles Manuscript Library
  Museum, Jacksonville, 86
Las Olas Art Show, Fort
  Lauderdale, 155
Museum of Fine Arts, 52
Museum of Art, Fort
  Lauderdale, 156
National Museum of Naval
  Aviation, Pensacola, 71
Quayside Market,
  Pensacola, 70
Royal Palm Gallery, Palm
  Beach, 126
Salvador Dali Museum, St.
  Petersburg, 11, 21
South Florida Historical
  Museum, Anna Maria
  Island, 29
Stuart Feed Supply, Stuart, 8
Ybor City State Museum,
  Ybor City, 101
AQUARIUMS
  The Pier, St. Petersburg, 22
  Marineland, Jacksonville, 86
  Sea World, Orlando, 89–90

BASEBALL
  Pittsburgh Pirates,
    Bradenton, 30
  Montreal Expos, Palm
    Beach, 92
  Atlanta Braves, Palm Beach,
    92

BOATS, CRUISES, CHARTERS
  Bahia Mar Boat Show, Fort
    Lauderdale, 155
  Big Red Boats of Premier
    Cruise Lines, 149–151
  Everglades National Park
    District, West Palm
    Beach, 120–121
  Houseboating, 103
  The Jungle Queen, Key
    Biscayne, 156
  Kahlua Cup Regatta,
    Clearwater, 11
  The Love Boat, 108
  Miss Cortez, Egmont Key,
    30
  Princess Ships, Fort
    Lauderdale, 108

CAFES, RESTAURANTS, PUBS
  Ashley's, Stuart, 9
  Beacon's Bistro, South
    Beach, 129
  Bon Appetit, Dunedin, 27
  Brown Derby, Orlando, 38
  Cafe Alcatraz, Orlando, 39
  Cafe Milano, South Beach,
    129
  Chili Pepper, South Beach,
    129
  Cocoa Beach Pier, Cocoa
    Beach, 97
  Columbia, Ybor City, 99

The Conch Train, Key West, 142

The Corner Cafe, Ybor City, 100

The Drawbridge Cafe, Belle Glade, 3

The El Pasaje Plaza/Cherokee Club, Ybor City, 100

Florida House, Amelia Island, 67

Joe's Stone Crab, South Beach, 129

The Jolly Sailor, Stuart, 9

Larios, South Beach, 129

La Tropicana Cafe, Ybor City, 99

Louie's, Orlando, 39

Louie's Backyard, Key West, 142

Louis Pappa's Riverside, Tarpon Springs, 19

Nick's, South Beach, 129

North Turn Restaurant, Daytona, 32

Pepe's, Key West, 142

Two Sisters, Coral Gables, 123

Shabeen, South Beach, 129

Shorty's Diner, Key West, 142

Schwab's Pharmacy, Orlando, 39

1878 Steak House, Amelia Island, 67

Victoria & Alberts, Orlando, 51

The Yearling, Cross Creek, 79

Yuca, Coral Gables, 123

CAMPGROUNDS, MARINAS, PARKS

BelleGlade Marina & Campground, 3

Blue Spring State Park, Palatka, 103

Bulow Plantation State Historic Site, 6

Cape Florida State Park, Key Biscayne, 145

Cape Florida Lighthouse, Key Biscayne, 145

Castle Park, Bradenton, 30

Cayo Costa Island State Preserve, 75

Cedar Keys National Wildlife Refuge, 74

Clewiston KOA, Clewiston, 4

Collier-Seminole State Park, Naples, 118

Crandon Park, Key Biscayne, 145

Cypress Gardens, Winter Haven, 61

Everglades National Park
  District, West Palm
  Beach, 120–121
Fort Clinch State Park,
  Amelia Island, 68
Gulf Islands National
  Seashore, Panhandle,
  71
Hontoon Landing Resort
  and Marina, Hontoon
  Island, 105
Lake Kissimmee State Park,
  Kissimmee, 46
Okeechobee KOA, 3
Silver Springs, Okala, 25
Sugar Mill Gardens, Port
  Orange, 5
CANOEING
Everglades, 63–64
Everglades National Park
  District, West Palm
  Beach, 120–121
Jonathan Dickinson State
  Park, 159
Long Key State Recreation
  Area, 159
Loxahatchee National
  Wildlife Refuge, 159
Treetops Park, Davie,
  159
West Lake Park, 159
CANAVERAL NATIONAL
  SEASHORE
Playalinda Beach, 97

CEREMONIES, FESTIVALS
Caribbean Calypso Festival,
  St. Petersburg, 22
Epiphany Celebration,
  Tarpon Springs, 20
CRACKER FARE
The Drawbridge Cafe, Belle
  Glade, 3

DINOSAURS
Sugar Mill Gardens, Port
  Orange, 6

ETHNIC
Greek, Tarpon Springs,
  19
Scottish Tatoo, Dunedin,
  26
Latin American, Ybor City,
  101

FERRIES
La Cruise, Jacksonville, 86
Mayport Ferry, Jacksonville,
  86
FISHING GUIDES
Bassfishing, St. John's River,
  35–37
FOOTBALL
Florida-Georgia game,
  Jacksonville, 85

The Outback Steakhouse
  Gator Bowl Classic,
  Jacksonville, 85
FRUIT
  Picking, 53–54

GOLF
  Amelia Island Plantation,
    Amelia Island, 69
  Belle Glade Marina &
    Campground, Belle
    Glade, 3
  Doral Golf Resort and Spa,
    Miami, 137–139
  Indian River Plantation,
    Stuart, 7
  The Links of Key Biscayne,
    Key Biscayne, 143
  Royal Caribbean Senior
    PGA Golf Classic, Key
    Biscayne, 143
  Silver Springs Rodeo,
    Kissimmee, 46
GREYHOUND RACING
  Information, 13–15

HALIFAX RIVER, 5
HERBERT HOOVER DIKE,
  Clewiston, 3
HIKING and BIKING
  Bike the Keys, 158
  Caladesi Island, 26

Cedar Key Scrub, Cedar
  Key, 74
Devil's Millhopper,
  Gainesville, 78
DuPuis Reserve State Forest,
  158
Everglades National Park
  District, West Palm
  Beach, 120–121
Fern Forest, 158
Florida Trail, 159
Fort Clinch State Park,
  Amelia Island, 68
Hungryland Boardwalk,
  Palm Beach Gardens, 159
Jonathan Dickinson State
  Park, 159
The Lake Okeechobee Trail,
  158
Long Key State Recreation
  Area, 159
Loxahatchee National
  Wildlife Refuge, 159
Ravine Gardens, Palatka,
  103
Sebastian Inlet State
  Recreation Area, 97
Shell Mound Park, Cedar
  Key, 74
West Lake Park, 159
HISTORICAL
  Amelia Island, 67
  Avondale Historic District
    Site, Jacksonville, 86–87

Archaelogical site, Miami,
113
Braden Castle, Bradenton, 30
Bronson-Mulholland House,
Palatka, 103
Bulow Plantation State
Historic Site, Daytona, 6
Cigars, Ybor City, Tampa,
99
Fort Caroline, Jacksonville,
87
The Frank Stranahan Home,
Fort Lauderdale, 156
The Goodland Fish House,
Marco Island, 153
Hernando De Soto Camp,
Anna Maria Island, 29
Key West, 140
Kingsley Plantation,
Jacksonville, 87
Manatee Village Historic
Park, Bradenton, 30
Micanopy, 79
Roaring Twenties, 7
San Marcos de Apalache
State Historic Site,
Apalachicola, 81
Seminole wars, 1, 5
Sponge Exchange, Tarpon
Springs, 19
Springfield Historic District,
Jacksonville, 86
Sugar Mill Ruins, New
Smyrna Beach, 6

Timucuan Ecological and
Historic Preserve,
Jacksonville, 87
Vintage Rail Depot, Waldo,
80
HISTORIC INNS
Artist House, Key West, 141
Curry Mansion, Key West,
141
Duval House, Key West, 141
Key West Bed & Breakfast,
Key West, 141
The Marquesa, Key West,
141
Miami River Inn, East Little
Havana, 113
Snook Inn, Old Marco, 153
HORSES
Horse Country, 23
Horseback riding, Ocala,
25
Lippizzan Stallions,
Bradenton, 30
HORSEBACK TRAILS
Treetops Park, Davie, 159
INDIAN SITES
Shell Mound Park, Cedar
Key, 74
Marco Island, 152–153

INFORMATION
Adopt a Greyhound
Program, 15

Alachua County Visitors
and Convention Bureau,
80
American Greyhound Track
Operators Association, 15
American Water Ski
Association, 61
Busch Gardens, Tampa, 17
Chamber of Commerce,
Apalachicola, 83
Chamber of Commerce,
Cedar Key, 74
Chamber of Commerce,
Dunedin, 28
Chamber of Commerce,
Fernandina Beach, 69
Chamber of Commerce,
Marco Island, 154
Chamber of Commerce,
Ocala, 25
Chamber of Commerce,
Pensacola, 72
Chamber of Commerce,
Stuart, 9
Chamber of Commerce,
Tarpon Springs, 20
Convention and Visitors
Bureau, Fort Lauderdale,
157
Convention and Visitors
Bureau, Jacksonville,
87
Convention and Visitors
Bureau, Tampa, 101

Daytona Convention and
Visitors Bureau, 6, 33
Development Department,
City of Coral Gables, 124
Florida Adventures Inc., 65
Florida Endowment for
Humanities, 3
Florida Department of
Natural Resources,
Tallahassee, 91
Florida Thoroughbred
Breeders Association, 23
Florida Tourism, 64
Florida Trails, 160
Florida Vacation Guide
from Florida Tourism, 57
Greater Miami Convention
and Visitors Bureau, 130
Lake Kissimmee State Park,
48
Lee County Visitor and
Convention Bureau,
148
Manatee County
Convention & Visitors
Bureau, 31
Naples Area Tourism
Bureau, 119
Natural Resources Office, 3
Palm Beach County Visitors
Guide, 94
Palm Beach County
Convention and Visitors
Bureau, 127

Southwest Volusia Chamber of Commerce, 6
Space Coast Office of Tourism, Viera, 98
St. Petersburg/Clearwater Area Convention & Visitors Bureau, 22
U. Gather Directory, 55
World Waterpark Association, 57
INNS, BED & BREAKFASTS, HOTELS
Archibald, Jacksonville, 86
Best Western Jamaican Inn, Dunedin, 27
Boca Raton Hotel and Club, Boca Raton, 92
The Breakers, Palm Beach, 92
Clewiston Inn, Clewiston, 2
Deland Country Inn, Deland, 37
The Gibson Inn, Apalachicola, 81
Josephine's Bed & Breakfast Inn, Seaside, 58
Live Oak Inn, Daytona, 34
Miami River Inn, East Little Havana, 113
Ocean Grand, Palm Beach, 92
Ritz Carlton, Palm Beach, 92
Seven Sisters Inn, Ocala, 25

South Beach, 128
Spring Bayou, Tarpon Springs, 20
St. John's House, Jacksonville, 85
INTERNATIONAL SWIMMING HALL OF FAME, Fort Lauderdale, 156
ISLANDS
Amelia Island, 66
Anna Maria, 29
Caladesi Island, 26
Cayo Costa Island, 75
Cedar Key, 73
Coral Gables, 122
The Dry Tortugas, 131
Honeymoon Island, 27
Hontoon Island, 104
Key Biscayne, 143
Longboat Key, 29
Marco Island, 152
Pine Island Sound, 146–147

KEY WEST SEAPLANE SERVICE, 133
KISSIMMEE RIVER BASIN, 1
KLASSIX CAR MUSEUM, 32
KRAVITZ CENTER FOR THE PERFORMING ARTS, Palm Beach, 93

LAKE OKEECHOBEE, 1
LIVING HISTORY
  Cow Camp, Kissimmee, 46
  Fort Pickens, Pensacola,
    71
  Seville Historic District,
    Pensacola, 70
  Silver Springs Rodeo,
    Kissimmee, 46
  A Walk Through Time,
    Gainesville, 78

MANATEES
  Habitat, 88
  Homosassa Springs State
    Wildlife Park, 90
  Lowry Park Zoo, Tampa,
    90
MOVIE STUDIOS
  MGM Disney Studios,
    Orlando, 38
  Universal Studios, Orlando,
    39
MUSEUMS. *See* ART
    MUSEUMS AND
    GALLERIES
MUSEUM OF DISCOVERY &
    SCIENCE, Fort
    Lauderdale, 156

NASA Kennedy Space Center,
    Cape Canaveral, 95

PALM BEACH POLO AND
    COUNTRY CLUB, 92
PANHANDLE COUNTRY,
    70–71

RACETRACKS
  Daytona International
    Speedway, Daytona, 32
RECREATIONAL VEHICLES
  Great Outdoors, Titusville,
    95
RESORTS/HOTELS
  Belleview Mido Resort
    Hotel, St. Petersburg, 10
  Boca Raton Hotel and Club,
    Boca Raton, 127
  Club Med Sandpiper, Port
    Lucie, 43, 45
  Colony Hotel, Tampa, 18
  Doral Golf Resort and Spa,
    Miami, 137–139
  Don CeSar Beach Resort, St.
    Petersburg, 10
  Embassy Suites, Stuart, 9
  Grand Floridian, Orlando,
    51
  Hotel Place St. Michel,
    Coral Gables, 122
  Indian River Plantation
    Resort, Hutchinson
    Island, 7, 9, 45
  Innisbrook, Tarpon Springs,
    20

Little Palm Island, Key
West, 141
Perry's Ocean-Edge,
Daytona, 34
Ritz-Carlton, Naples, 118
Seaside Village Community,
Tallahassee, 58
Sonesta Beach Resort, Key
Biscayne, 143
Stouffer Vinoy, St.
Petersburg, 10, 21
Turnberry Isle Resort and
Club, Aventura, 135

SCUBA DIVING
Kings Bay, 88
Palm Beach, 93
SEA KAYAKING, 65
SHOPPING
Bal Harbour,South Beach,
129
Bayside Festival
Marketplace, Miami, 114
Calle Ocho Latin area,
Miami, 113
Cocoa Village, Cocoa
Beach, 95
Delectable Collectibles,
Micanopy, 80
The Pier, St. Petersburg, 11
Rare Earth Pottery, Stuart, 8
The Post Office Arcade,
Stuart, 8

Sawgrass Outlet Mall, Fort
Lauderdale, 155
Sponge Exchange, 19
Village Square Book Shop,
Micanopy, 79
Worth Avenue, Boca Raton,
126
Ybor City, Tampa, 99
ST. JOHN'S RIVER, 90, 103
SWAMP BUGG
CHAMPIONSHIP RACES,
Naples, 119

THEATER, DANCE
Alhambra Dinner Theater,
Jacksonville, 86
Boca Raton Ballet Theater
Company, 125
Caldwell Theater, Boca
Raton, 125
Performing Arts Center,
Fort Lauderdale, 155
Royal Palm Dinner Theater,
Boca Raton, 125
Royal Poinciana Playhouse,
Boca Raton, 125
THEME PARKS
Busch Gardens, Tampa, 16
Cypress Gardens, Winter
Haven, 61
Walt Disney World,
Orlando, 38, 50
Sea World, Orlando, 89–90

TOWNS & CITIES
  Apalachicola, 81
  Aventura, 135
  Belle Glade, 2
  Boca Raton, 125
  Cape Canaveral, 7
  Clearwater, 10
  Clewiston, 2
  Cocoa Beach, 95
  Coral Gables, 122
  Cross Creek, 79
  Cypress Gardens, 60
  Daytona, 5, 32
  Deland, 35
  Dunedin, 26
  Dry Tortugas, 131
  Fort Lauderdale, 155
  Gainesville, 78
  Gold Coast, 7
  Jacksonville, 85
  Key Biscayne, 143
  Key West, 140
  Kissimmee, 46, 106
  Miami, 111, 137, 143
  Micanopy, 79
  Naples, 117
  New Smyrna Beach, 5
  Ocala, 22
  Okeechobee, 1–4
  Orlando, 38
  Palm Beach, 92–94
  Pensacola, 70
  Port Orange, 5
  Port Lucie, 43

  Seaside, 58
  South Beach, 128
  St. Augustine, 5
  St. Petersburg, 9, 21
  Stuart, 7
  Tarpon Springs, 19
  Winter Haven, 61
  Ybor City, Tampa, 99
TRAINS
  Lolly the Trolley (tour), Fort
    Lauderdale, 156
  Old Train Trolley, Key West,
    142

UNIVERSITY OF FLORIDA,
  Gainesville, 78

WALT DISNEY WORLD,
  Orlando, 57
WATER PARKS
  Adventure Island, Tampa, 56
  Blizzard Beach, Walt Disney
    World, Orlando, 57
  River Country, Walt Disney
    World, Orlando, 57
  Typhoon Lagoon, Walt
    Disney World, Orlando,
    57
  Weeki Wachee, 57
WATER SKIING
  American Water Ski
    Association, 61

Water Ski Hall of Fame,
  Winter Haven, 61
WEDDINGS, VOW RENEWAL
  CEREMONIES
Vow renewal ceremony,
  Walt Disney World,
  50–52
WILDLIFE REFUGES, PARKS,
  PRESERVES,
Blue Spring State Park,
  Palatka, 103
Big Cypress Swamp, 117
Cedar Key National
  Wildlife Refuge, 74
Conservancy Nature Center,
  Naples, 118
Everglades, 117
Fairchild Tropical Garden,
  Coral Gables, 123
Homosassa Springs State
  Wildlife Park, 90
Indian River Lagoon, 97

Lake Woodruff Bird
  Sanctuary, Palatka, 104
Marco Island, 152
Matheson Hammock Park,
  Coral Gables, 123
Merritt Island National
  Wildlife Refuge, 97
National Audubon Society
  Sanctuary, Naples, 117
Paynes Prairie State
  Preserve, Gainesville, 78
Rookery Bay National
  Estuarine Research
  Reserve, Naples, 118
St. Vincent National
  Wildlife Refuge,
  Apalachicola, 82
Timucuan Ecological and
  Historic Preserve,
  Jacksonville, 87
Waccasassa Bay State
  Preserve, 74